INDIAN MINIATURE PAINTING

Jammu
Mankot
Jasrota
Basohli
Lahore
Kangra
Kulu
Guler
Delhi
Bikaner
Sanganer
RAJASTHAN
Alwar
Agra
Lucknow
Kishangarh
Jaipur
Jodhpur
Ajmer
Gwalior
Jaunpur
Patna
Pali
Shahpura
Datia
Bundi
Benares
Kotah
BUNDELKHAND
Sirohi
Nathdwara
Murshidabad
Udaipur
Orchha
Partagarh
Patan
Narsinghgarh
Calcutta
GUJARAT
MALWA
Ahmedabad
Mandu
Pari (Orissa)
Ajanta
Ellora
BAY OF BENGAL
Ahmednagar
Bombay
Bidar
Hyderabad
ARABIAN SEA
Bijapur
Badrini
Madras
Kanchipuram
Mysore
Tanjore
Sittanavasal
CEYLON

Indian Miniature Painting

THE COLLECTION OF

EARNEST C. AND JANE WERNER WATSON

PUBLISHED BY THE ELVEHJEM ART CENTER

UNIVERSITY OF WISCONSIN, MADISON

DISTRIBUTED BY THE UNIVERSITY OF

WISCONSIN PRESS, MADISON

Published 1971
The Elvehjem Art Center

Distributed by
The University of Wisconsin Press
Box 1379, Madison, Wisconsin 53701

The University of Wisconsin Press, Ltd.
70 Great Russell Street, London, W.C.1

The exhibition and catalogue were
supported by a generous grant from
the Thomas E. Brittingham Trust

Designed by Richard Hendel

Printed in the United States of America
ISBN 0-299-97005-1; LC 70-157396

In Memoriam

Earnest Charles Watson

HONORARY PATRONS

HIS EXCELLENCY, L.K. JHA, *Ambassador of India to the United States of America*

HIS EXCELLENCY, KENNETH B. KEATING, *Ambassador of the United States of America to India*

JOHN KENNETH GALBRAITH, *Harvard University*

V.K. AHUJA, *Consul General of India, New York*

P. GANGULEE, *Minister (Education and Culture), Embassy of India*

MR. AND MRS. PHILLIPS TALBOT, *President, The Asia Society*

MR. AND MRS. DOUGLAS ENSMINGER, *University of Missouri*

CONTENTS

Foreword

MILLARD F. ROGERS, JR.
Director

A "MINIATURE" PAINTING refers to one small in size and delicate in brushwork. Between the sixteenth and mid-nineteenth centuries, European and American artists produced miniature paintings. They were portraits, usually, meant to be appreciated rather privately. But this art form was never as popular as painting on a larger format. Most easel pictures, wall frescoes, and painted ceilings familiar to Western eyes can be appreciated by one, or five, or fifty viewers at one time. A miniature painting is meant to be seen by a single viewer, although modern museum practice tends to exhibit it so that several viewers may see it simultaneously. This is a fundamental difference between it and other types of painting.

Indian miniature paintings were intended for contemplation, instruction, or enjoyment by one individual at a time. They were decorated sheets in portfolios or books, held on the lap or table for study. Originally, they were not framed behind glass or exhibited on walls. Indian artists worked within a patronage system of courtly schools and ateliers, and their paintings were not done often for those outside the court. Except for some paintings on palm leaf and animal membrane, soft paper (sometimes compressed into thin pads) is the support on which the artist painted with gouache—opaque colors ground in water and mixed with a gum preparation. There were specialists who painted the decorative borders and mountings, and the skillful copying of older masterpieces was not considered odious to Indian aesthetics.

This splendid array of Indian miniature paintings is the collection of Mr. and Mrs. Earnest C. Watson, formed by them as a gift to the Elvehjem Art Center. Their generosity in support of our permanent art collection parallels their love of Indian art and culture. Jane Werner Watson is an alumna of the University, and it has been the Watsons' pleasure and our great honor to have been selected as the home for this collection. One of the most important private collections in America, this group deserves the recognition and scholarship now provided by this catalogue. The research, published catalogue, and exhibition were financed by a generous grant from the Thomas E. Brittingham Trust, and we gratefully acknowledge this support and that of members of the Brittingham family. We thank the individuals who have graciously consented to serve as patrons.

We are indebted to Professor Pramod Chandra of the University of Chicago who accepted our invitation to conduct research on the Watson collection of Indian miniature paintings and to prepare this catalogue. His scholarship and expertise have provided the interpretive record of this group of paintings.

Several fine catalogues of private collections or exhibitions of Indian miniature painting have appeared since the publication of the catalogue of Śrī Motichand Khajanchi's collections, on which Professor Chandra worked with Moti Chandra and Karl Khandalavala. These catalogues include the poetically titled *Gods, Thrones and Peacocks* by Stuart C. Welch and Milo C. Beach; *Rajput Miniatures* by the collector Edwin Binney III and W.G. Archer; Mr. Welch's catalogue of the splendid New York exhibition of Mughal art; and several other catalogues of smaller exhibitions. They have added much to the corpus of published paintings, and their authors have taken great interest in introducing the subject to the reader.

The assistance of friends and colleagues of Professor Chandra who helped with the catalogue, including Stuart C. Welch, Robert Skelton, W.G. Archer, B.N. Goswamy and Chaudary Muhammad Naim, is appreciated. The Elvehjem Art Center staff has assisted the entire project through many difficult stages. Many details were handled by Arthur R. Blumenthal, Curator, and John S. Hopkins, Registrar. Preparation of the paintings for exhibition and editorial assistance have been provided by Carlton Overland, Project Assistant. Publicity was prepared by Mrs. Catherine Brawer; editorial assistance, typing, and administrative matters were in the capable hands of Mrs. Ruth A. Jackson and Mrs. Pamela Rosenthal. Carpentry and installation problems were solved by staff carpenter, Henry Behrnd. The photography of the paintings was done by Harold Clason of Santa Barbara, California, and David Spradling, Madison, Wisconsin. The catalogue was designed by Richard Hendel of Amherst, Massachusetts. In this catalogue, illustration numbers refer to catalogue entry numbers.

This catalogue includes nearly all of the paintings in the Watson collection with the exception of a few non-Indian works acquired originally for their stylistic relationships. Every painting listed in this catalogue was exhibited at the Elvehjem Art Center during the initial showing of the Watson collection.

I will always have a special affection for this collection of paintings, for the exhibition and catalogue, but especially for Jane and Earnest Watson. It was the first donor contact I made after my appointment as Director in 1967, and it is the first major exhibition organized by the Elvehjem Art Center following its Inaugural Exhibition. The cooperation of the Watsons during the planning of this exhibition and catalogue was never lacking, and the University of Wisconsin is deeply grateful to them. The Elvehjem Art Center has designated this exhibition and catalogue as a memorial tribute to the late Earnest Charles Watson and records its sorrow at his passing.

Journey into the Little World of Kṛishṇa

The Collecting of Indian Miniatures

JANE WERNER WATSON

WE DIDN'T INTEND to collect Indian miniature paintings. In fact, when, with Earnest's assignment as science attaché to the United States Embassy in New Delhi, we contemplated a stay of two years or more in India, we rather definitely planned for a change not to collect anything. At the words "Indian arts" in those days all that flashed into our minds' eyes were frenetic bronze figures of strange divinities waving multitudinous arms in all directions. To those we felt our resistance would be really high, and it did prove to be, even when our feeling of strangeness toward Indian gods had given way to a certain respectful familiarity.

All we intended to do at the start was to make the cavernous rooms of our furnished flat in Delhi livable. An eighteen-foot-wide linen scroll block-printed mainly in carmine and viridian green soon warmed one vast, blank, whitewashed wall. A life-sized head chiseled from rough greenish schist by a craftsman of the Kushan period almost two thousand years ago gazed confidently from the mantel. A *hukkā* of painted marble and clay awaited the moment when we might long for a puff or two of water-cooled tobacco smoke. And a jumbo wine jug of minutely engraved silver purportedly made for a lieutenant of Akbar, greatest of the Mughal emperors, lent a grand air to our otherwise undistinguished library table.

Then we encountered an old silver *pān* or *kemam* box with the airy grace of a crown for a princess. Its circle of small sectional boxes—for the various nuts and spices to be wrapped in a shiny green betel leaf, pinned with a clove, and tucked into the cheek as an after-dinner delicacy—was raised on curved legs, topped with water sapphires, and inlaid with birds and flowers. These small forms glowed with the brilliance of the powdered emeralds and deep blue sapphires that we were told (erroneously, I'm afraid) went into the making of the enamel. The *pān* box soon reposed on the battered rented grand piano that, incidentally, had been delivered to us on an ox cart manned by a crew of thirteen eager, bumbling youngsters.

Once we had an example of this fairly rare enamel on silver, we began to feel a growing yearning for a bit of old Mughal enamel on gold. This purchase involved a good deal of shopping around. As we crouched on one of the low plush divans to be found in the inner chambers of many Delhi jewelers, a soft-voiced proprietor would cause to materialize from some secret recess a sequence of leather cases. Placed one at a time on the table before us, as the dealer flicked a catch with the air of a necromancer, each case would open to disclose within a glowing treasure embedded in velvet or sunk in puffs of silk.

Having marveled at golden chess pawn soldiers uniformed in satiny enamel, at graceful small boxes from whose covers smiled enameled portraits of court beauties, at a green enamel parrot whose golden claws tipped in ruby enamel clutched a golden perch and from whose beak royal lips had once sipped wine, we began to feel faintly imperial ourselves. We half settled on a gold locket with handsome enamel portraits inside and out, but a purchase of this magnitude seemed to merit a bit of thinking over. We retired without committing ourselves; and when we returned after a lapse of a couple of weeks it was to find that we had lost the locket to the Cleveland Museum of Art. Our final choice was a pachisi set whose playing pieces were shaped like chocolate drops but made of gold, spangled with tiny leaves and flowers of ruby, emerald and amethyst enamel; its dice were long and lean as small golden flower-spangled bones.

By this time a project was taking shape in our minds. We decided it would be fun to assemble for some then undetermined museum in the United States examples of the principal decorative art forms of India. We have since settled upon the Elvehjem Art Center at the University of Wisconsin as the collection's permanent home.

We had our engraved silver, our enamel on silver and on gold. Now we added an eighteenth-century book cover of lacquered wood painted with the ten incarnations of the god Vishṇu; a Rājasthānī painted jewel box embellished with lively folk figures; a small bowl of mottled spinach jade inlaid with satin-smooth agates, turquoises and carnelians in the style of the inlaid marble of the Taj Mahal. And when one day one of our dealer friends, hushed with awe, laid in my hands a miniature bronze Vishṇu shrine of the Pāla school of a thousand years ago, three inches high with an inch-and-a-quarter tall Vishṇu exquisitely modeled, it proved irresistible too.

Now it seemed only natural to add to these an example of the Indian miniature paintings that flourished from the late sixteenth through the mid-nineteenth centuries. One of our favorite dealers called one day to say that he had just acquired a dozen particularly fine old Rajput paintings from the princely state of Bundi. He had been trying for several years to get these and he very much wanted us to see them while he had them all.

Saturday mornings when we were in Delhi, we customarily went on a round of shopping errands, so the following Saturday we strolled through the morning quiet of New Delhi to Sunder Nagar market. There we were ushered into a darkened shop by the bowing, smiling young doorkeeper. Inside there was a scurrying while the dealer's assistant padded about turning on lights. Then the curtain leading to the small office at the rear was swept aside, and in stepped the young dealer, his face alight with pleasure.

In response to a quick word, his elderly servant ducked down behind a low partition to reappear with an armload wrapped in silk. The wrappings were unfolded to disclose at last a dozen paintings, roughly seven by eleven inches in size, mounted on heavy paper. As we bent over them we entered for the first time the little world of Kṛishṇa, the wonderworld of Indian miniatures.

Not all Indian miniatures relate directly

to Kṛishṇa worship, of course. The earliest small paintings done on paper with mineral pigments in India illustrated scriptures of the Jain religion, and were in turn an outgrowth of earlier illuminated Buddhist manuscripts on strips of palm leaf. In the sixteenth century, Moslem invaders from the northwest brought the tradition of Persian painting to their courts in India and developed workshops where skilled craftsmen illustrated old tales and portrayed scenes of courtly life in fresh styles known now as Deccanī and Mughal. All these antedated the development of the most truly Indian Rajput tradition, which spread and flourished as one expression of the many-faceted artistic renaissance spurred by a resurgence of worship of the god Vishṇu (one of the central trinity of Hinduism) in the form of Lord Kṛishṇa.

All that we were to learn later. For the moment we simply succumbed to the brilliance and enchantment of the small scenes. One of the two we selected was from a set of the sort called *barah masa*, painted to illustrate the seasons of the Indian year. This one honored the coming of the monsoon season, which brings to the north Indian plains relief from months of searing dry heat and is consequently greeted with passionate delight.

In our painting, night has fallen and against an inky sky heavy with a burden of wallowing clouds golden snakes of lightning slither. A garden fountain sends its lacy water fronds leaping to welcome the coming rain, and in a pergola Lord Kṛishṇa and his lady love Rādhā sway in a vine-and-tree embrace, while overhead a snug chamber with couch spread in cloth of gold awaits their pleasure.

Our second acquisition was, we were told, one of a set called a *rāgamālā*, garland of melody. These were done to illustrate the classical Indian musical modes, the *ragas* and *rāginīs*, visualized as princes and their consorts. In our painting a lady and her handmaidens sit at ease on a richly decorated palace terrace, while behind them, against a sky of deepest lapis lazuli blue, pairs of birds flirt sweetly in a waterfall of foliage.

Now we had our sampling of the art of miniature painting, we told ourselves. Once the pair had been matted in raw silk, framed in narrow strips of teak and hung above my desk in our sun-bright morning room, we eyed them with satisfaction and breathed a small sigh of accomplishment. That, we thought innocently, was that.

We did casually acquire a few pages from an old manuscript of the desert state of Jodhpur, rather appealingly illustrated with plump and pompous courtiers and ladies. After all, bookmaking represented a rather different art, didn't it? In this connection, it seemed only sensible to have a page from one of those old books of Jain scriptures, too; the one we chose dated probably from the sixteenth century, its figures drawn in a typical nervous, spidery line and colored with deep red, rich blue and gold.

These duly assimilated, we went staunchly back to our sampling of various forms and materials, adding a haughty village dancing girl of warm old ivory, a gourd-shaped South Indian jewel box of painted wood, a silver fan hung with tiny tinkling bells, some chessmen and pachisi players in painted ivory, and other game pieces and small figures in bone, silver, mutton-fat jade—and so on.

It happened, however, that the door-to-door peddler who came with the ivory dancing girl also had a stack of paintings to offer. Since he came with a *chit*, a note from a friend of ours, I felt duty bound to glance through them simply as a courtesy. In the batch was a very small, infinitely delicate portrait of a wistful young woman seated under a flowering tree among whose leaves were hidden almost invisible pairs of parakeets, while against the high clouds above streaked a hair-fine flight of cranes.

The painting came, we were told, from Bikaner, a one-time princely state on the western desert to which a number of painters from the imperial court of the Mughals had migrated. Surely there was no harm in humoring ourselves with one more old painting, one so very slender and heart-touching?

And, on another Saturday round, a dealer showed us, just in passing, an especially fine Kangra miniature. It pictured Lord Kṛishṇa leading Rādhā down a meadow path by night, under tree branches afoam with white blossoms symbolic of dawning passion, beside a pool studded with pink lotuses of ethereal purity, under the bland and innocent gaze of a sacred milk-white cow and calf. All symbolism aside, it struck us as a charming little painting in its own right, the figures graceful and tender, their costumes a soft glow of yellow and orange against the warm gray mystery of the night. We liked it; and it did after all represent quite a different area and artistic tradition from our other miniatures, for the Kangra Valley in the Himalayan foothills had been the site of the development, in the mid-eighteenth century, of the last major school of Rajput painting. Wasn't its purchase, we asked ourselves plaintively, perhaps justifiable?

At that stage, you see, we were still rationalizing, still justifying, still tilting our rather battered small tin swords of logic against the huge, relentless windmill arms of the collecting urge blown by the winds of overweaning curiosity.

It was curiosity that made us expose ourselves to miniatures by the hundreds and thousands in the museums of India, curiosity that led me to leaf attentively through paintings by the score—more often the hundred—in the frequently dusty and unpromising packs of dealers who, alerted by the grapevine of their trade, found their way to our door, if we did not find our way to theirs.

One of my favorites was an elderly gentleman from a remote desert village. In he would shuffle under the disapproving eye of our bearer, followed by a servant—sometimes a grandson in training—carrying a bulky cloth-wrapped bundle or tottering under a heavy tin trunk with clanking padlock. Down he would sink, cross-legged on the morning room floor—scorning our lumpy overstuffed chairs—sandals kicked off for greater comfort. Then, with an elegance of gesture that promised the treasures of Aladdin, cloth wrappings or trunk tops would be flung back, and out the paintings would come.

As we fingered the precious papers and peered, with the aid of a reading glass when details were really minute, checking tempting offerings against a growing pile of reference books, our eyes became more keenly aware. And as the piles of rupees we had counted out here and there mounted, we began to react in accordance with Watson's Law. This law, one of the principal fruits of my husband's long extra-curricular career as a collector, runs as follows: If you want to learn about anything, invest in it. Having invested, we read and compared, asked questions and made notes.

Our dealer friends were most helpful, more eager, it seemed, to share their wealth of knowledge with someone whose interest was genuine than to make a sale. With one in particular we have developed over the years a warm familial relationship. How many quiet hours of rich delight I have spent bent over a table in the mezzanine room above his shop, the stacks of paintings passing under my hands constantly replenished by a khaki-clad helper who also conjured up at intervals a cola drink or tea. When I had made a preliminary selection for further study and conference at home, the dealer always found time to answer my questions, drawing upon background knowledge of truly scholarly breadth and depth. His contribution to this collection, in terms of information, guidance, warm interest and other assistance has been a major one. So it was that gradually, with the aid of men like this and in the course of acquiring many more paintings than we had ever dreamed even of admiring, we learned something about Indian miniatures.

We learned that each of dozens of princely courts had its own corps of painters, particularly during the seventeenth and eighteenth centuries. Thanks to the rigid discipline of a hereditary craft complete with model sheets to be memorized, each atelier, isolated by feudal rivalries and limited communication, developed its own recognizable style. The artists remained with few exceptions anonymous, but each local school came to have intriguingly individual mannerisms.

As we became increasingly interested in these local styles, interrelated but distinct, we reached another conclusion. Surely, we told ourselves, it was only sensible to put together while they were still readily available in the Delhi market samplings of all these schools, representing wherever possible the major stages in their development—and even decline.

Sensible or not, that is what we tried to do through the two and a half years of our residence in Delhi from early 1960 until 1962. On each of our half dozen return visits during the years since, we have tried to fill some of the gaps in the coverage. Here is the result. We most warmly hope that it will provide for many of our friends a pleasant introduction to an enchanted land in which we have spent countless happy hours—the little world of Kṛishṇa in Indian miniatures.

Some Notes for Viewers

If we could consider the paintings together, these are some of the thoughts regarding the collection that I would like to share with you:

Since the earliest illustrated manuscripts done in India and extant today are Buddhist texts done on strips of palm leaf, we were pleased to be able to acquire a partial sheet from one of these old manuscripts (Catalogue no. 1) with two of its original three very small illustrations still visible.

This custom of inscribing manuscripts on palm-leaf strips continued in eastern states, from Orissa south to Tamilnad, into the nineteenth century. We acquired two leaves from a set, which an expert friend assured us dated to about 1600 (no. 7), offering delightful glimpses into life at an Orissan court; a nineteenth-century illustrated copy of the *Gīta Govinda*, a tale of Lord Kṛishṇa; and a battered manuscript from Tamilnad of interest mainly because it retains the coarse cords, threaded through holes in the palm leaves and tipped with conch shells, on which these books were customarily strung. (For a glimpse of a series of paintings on paper patterned after the palm-leaf pages, see no. 268.)

In the fourteenth century paper was introduced into India from China. Though fairly large sheets were available, bookmakers were timid about enlarging their format, at first venturing only to a page depth of about four inches in place of two. Illustrations were still confined to rigidly defined blocks. In our example, no. 2, a page perhaps from the *Panchatantra Tales* produced in the very early fifteenth century, illustrations are scarcely larger than they could have been on palm-leaf strips.

The first great surge of production in this new format was spurred by the threat to established Indian religions presented by Muslim invasions from the northwest. Wealthy devotees of Jainism, by commissioning elaborately illuminated and embellished copies of their scriptures, became patrons of the first major school of Indian miniature painting. We were fortunate enough to be able to acquire one sheet of a magnificently decorated manuscript, no. 3, as well as several other examples of Jain manuscript illustration (nos. 4, 5, and 6) whose illustrations, closely studied, yield a surprising amount of information as to costumes, decorative arts and even architecture of the period. Since the Jains base their worship on reverence for twenty-four saints, each associated with some animal or other device, we were pleased to find an unusual set of panels, no. 221, showing all the saints. We also acquired several other paintings with Jain subject matter: one, no. 92, shows the rarely pictured "sky-clad" devotees of the Dijamber sect; no. 148 is a temple scene; no. 84 a folktale illustration; no. 215 a micro-miniaturized processional scene probably from Bundi; no. 141 a crudely done but interesting page illustrating the symbols representing the fourteen auspicious dreams that appeared to the mother of the leading Jain saint before the birth of her child. With the addition of a complete manuscript of the adventures of *Śrī Pal*, including some illustrations of seagoing ships quite unusual in Indian painting, we felt that this sampling increased our insight into the lives of the small but influential Jain trading community during the fifteenth through the eighteenth centuries and also into the rise and decline of a vitally important school of Indian painting which was to exercise a strong influence on the development of the art at a number of Indian courts. We have tried to do the same sort of sampling for other regional schools.

While Jain manuscripts were being churned out, some of the raiding Muslim bands had settled down in India, establishing a number of Muslim Sultanates. These courts maintained trade contacts with Persia, and works of art were among their imports. Reflections of Persian art can be seen even in some Jain paintings, for example in the arabesques on one side of no. 3 and in the features of the king shown in no. 5. Some paintings done for Muslim rulers in Central India in the sixteenth century (and earlier) are so close to the Persian style that they are often referred to as Indo-Persian (see nos. 10, 11, 12).

Elements of the Persian style, such as a liking for formally handled masses or tufts of flowering plants and for pinkish-lavender scalloped rocks, continue to appear in paintings done at Muslim courts of the Deccan peninsula long after those states had fallen under the sway of the great Mughals. Thus the hesitant young ivory-skinned beauty being led to the harem by the aged one-time beauty in no. 69 is drawn in Mughal fashion, while the flowing line of Persian figure drawing can be seen, despite its very worn condition, in the small page (no. 60) probably from a "sleeve book" done at diamond-rich

Golconda, and in no. 62, probably done at the lavish court of Bijapur. I mention these local courts rather tentatively since not a great deal of scholarly work has as yet been done on the paintings of the Deccanī courts; and some scholars, including Dr. Pramod Chandra who has done the body of this catalogue, prefer to group paintings simply under area designations rather than to risk largely subjective attributions to local courts. However, since we found it stimulating at a puzzle-solving level to try to assign paintings to more specific locales and to sample in our collection as many as possible of these local schools, I shall mention some of our unproven but probable local identifications. For example, the dancing devotee of no. 62 strongly resembles in style the faint remnants of almost vanished wall paintings in a water pavilion we visited near Bijapur. Figures in no. 60 have much of this same fluid grace, but almost more strongly resemble the musicians and dancers of Golconda pictured on page 122 of the Skira *Paintings of India*. We also cling, for lack of negative evidence, to tentative identifications of the elegant gentlemen of no. 31 as of Mughal-period Golconda or its successor, Hyderabad; no. 144 has similarly been identified as belonging to the small Deccanī court of Kurnool; no. 72 is said to be from Poona; and the equestrian of no. 46 a noble of Arcot. (The crudely painted black buck, no. 53, on the reverse was an accidental acquisition.) The dancer on the garden terrace in no. 65 we also think of as a courtesan of Hyderabad, the city that succeeded Golconda as capital of that immensely wealthy state. The lavish riverside palace of no. 42 is certainly Deccanī, and this painting is unusual in being signed (look very closely at the center of the painting about a third of the way up from the bottom for the delicate Arabic characters) by a recognized Deccanī painter, Faizullah, so the National Museum in New Delhi assured us. The *simhāsana* or "lion throne" hanging, no. 218, was added to our collection to represent the elaborately painted cloths produced at several Deccanī centers to provide backdrops for and to decorate the bases beneath temple images.

The images were of course Hindu; Muslim artists in general seem to have been surprisingly willing to illustrate Hindu subject matter. This was particularly true at the Mughal court of Akbar the Great (1556–1605), a man of unusual breadth of mind, interested in all the religions of his complex empire. We like to think that no. 139, which came to us quite without pedigree through a door-to-door peddler, might show Akbar conversing with men of different faiths, as he liked to do.

Paintings produced in the workrooms of the imperial Mughal court, and the very attractive and competent work done at some of the provincial Mughal courts, have been sought after since the first European traders and travelers began to visit India in the sixteenth century. Today collectors who are determined to acquire sheets from the great historical and romantic manuscripts illustrated under Akbar, distinguished portraits and animal paintings done under Jahāngīr, or exquisite if less lively paintings of the Shāh Jahān reign must for the most part frequent galleries and auctions of London, New York and Paris and be prepared to invest major sums. Since we were collecting in India, where the market has long since been stripped of most of its outstanding Mughal paintings, and were buying from modest earned income, we did not attempt to compete in that sphere. However, over the period of a decade or more we did manage to acquire what we feel are creditable examples of the principal periods in both the rise and the decline of the Mughal style, and also of its wide range of subject matter.

First came the early Akbar-period page, no. 13, which a friend from the Metropolitan Museum identified as illustrating the tale of "the yak-yak tree." Probably no. 14 once was as brilliant a painting, but it has fallen on hard days during the past three centuries and now is interesting primarily for its subject and for certain classic features of composition such as the two balanced groups of six figures each. The subject is the birth of a prince; since the father figure receiving word of the birth is shown wearing a turban style generally associated with Humāyūn, father of Akbar, it is tempting to feel that the birth being celebrated pictorially may have been Akbar's own. Another acquisition that has brought us special pleasure is no. 15, which again we and highly knowledgeable friends identify with Akbar himself, since he delighted in riding his wild-spirited elephant Hawai at considerable risk to his royal person.

The exquisite small volume of the romance of Yūsuf and Zulaykhā — the Muslim version of the Biblical story of Joseph and Potiphar's wife, we are told — from which nos. 17 and 18 come, was evidently made during the early years of Jahāngīr's reign (1605–1627). These illustrations not only please us pictorially but are of interest as Mughal paintings firmly rooted in the Persian tradition: the flat, vertical perspective in which more distant groups simply appear above foreground figures, often separated by a wall or bank of foliage; the stylized flowering plants; the rather formal placement of figures. The Indian locale is equally clearly indicated, however, by the brilliance of the color and the unmistakably Indian costumes of the female figures.

Painting during Jahāngīr's reign is noted for portraiture, interest in birds and animals, and for a gradual gentling of palette. We felt fortunate to find the fine tinted sketch for an imperial portrait of Emperor Jahāngīr (no. 25) and the startlingly realistic hoopoe (no. 20), one of my husband's favorites among our paintings as the hoopoe was our favorite among India's marvelous birds.

As trade with Europe grew, European costumes came to hold a special fascination for the Mughals, and they delighted in having women of their harems painted in this exotic attire. They also assigned painters to the copying of Western paintings and engravings. We were pleased therefore to find the charming young lady seen in no. 24 pictured by a Mughal painter with an unfamiliar — to the artist — stemmed goblet precariously balanced on a circle of forefinger and thumb, and the slim and sophisticated Deccanī woman in no. 61, shown in the act of pouring wine. Incidentally, it seems highly possible that no. 61 was painted some years later than no. 62, and that they were later mounted back to back after the casual fashion in which many albums were assembled for private enjoyment. Pictures of assorted sizes and shapes were mounted on standard unbound album sheets and surrounded with decorative borders. Some artists, it appears, spent their entire careers in the production of these borders. We never had an opportunity to buy one of the particularly splendid album sheets with birds, flowers and human figures in full color scattered among the formal gold floral patterns, but the collection does contain several album sheets, including nos. 24, 29, 37, and nos. 63 and 64 mounted back to back. (No. 119 shows a Rajput version of one of these borders.)

The portrait of the Rajput noble in no. 29 is, we were assured by an expert, one of a series made for the great Mughal emperors as a part of their intelligence system, to acquaint them with the men with whom they might one day have to deal. It is interesting to compare the ivory-smooth skin of this figure with the stippled brushwork used in later Mughal paintings such as nos. 48–50 and no. 51.

The greatest period of Mughal painting came to an end with the reign of Aurangzeb, whose religious bigotry caused him to turn against all the arts. He is generally pictured bent over his holy *Koran*, as in nos. 30 and 49. Some time after we had bought no. 30, we happened upon a late nineteenth-century copy of it (no. 58). Whereas many of the background details of the early painting have chipped away, they can be clearly seen in the copy. This copy, like no. 59, shows the last stage in the decline of the Mughal style. Then old subjects were being quickly reproduced for a new market of foreigners. The painstaking process involving drawing the outline, sizing the paper, retracing the drawing, painting in flat areas of color, then superimposing details of costume and background had been abandoned in favor of a one-step process that produced work drained not only of all brilliance of color but of life itself.

Before this final breakdown, Mughal painting had enjoyed brief resurgences of both royal patronage and approach to brilliance under the pleasure-loving reigns of Muhammad Shāh (1719–1748), here represented by no. 39, and Shāh Ālam (1759–1806), represented by nos. 48–50 and 51. Scenes of courtly dalliance were the most favored subjects during these twilight eras.

The principal result of Aurangzeb's denial of the arts was to scatter the skilled masters of the imperial atelier, some to provincial courts such as Lucknow and Murshidabad (see nos. 36–38), some to the Pahāṛī or Hill states far to the north (see nos. 225–267), more to the Rajput feudal states where the most prolific and varied school of Indian painting developed.

There had been some illustrated manuscripts done at Rajput courts before Mughal influence reached them. Painters had picked up elements of style and tricks of technique from Gujarat to the west, a center of early Jain work (nos. 83–85), and perhaps from Malwa, a Central Indian Muslim kingdom to the east of Rajasthan, or Rajputana as it was then called (see nos. 130–134).

Malwa's painters had begun during the sixteenth century to combine elements of Jain, Persian and local folk styles to produce flat patterns, composed of boxy areas after the Jain style, in which figures were rather stiffly placed, the whole decorated with flowering tufts and bushes after the Persian fashion, and often with bands of Persian arabesque at the bottom. Despite all these borrowed characteristics, we were pleased to discover on a visit to the old Malwa capital of Mandu that some of the architectural details, such as very squat domes that often top some of the room "boxes" of the compositions, were evidently drawn from direct observation, as were the patterns of fabrics with their rich variety of designs. Even the palette, rather subdued by comparison with the rich, full-bodied pigments of Rajasthan, is reflected in the rose and blue fabrics one sees on many women of the area today.

The earliest Rajput paintings in our collection date from the same mid-seventeenth-century decades as our early Malwas. The Rajput works are also two-dimensional (see no. 83); some (no. 88) have groups of figures enclosed in boxes formed by architectural elements or foliage, in others (see no. 142) rows of figures are ranged along a base line against flat color.

It is difficult, as has been mentioned in connection with work done in the

Deccanī kingdoms and as will later be found true in the northern Hill states, to be very definite about the sites of the workshops in which many of the paintings were produced. Again it has been a puzzle-solving project for us, armed with reference books and backed by many hours of museum browsing, to try to bolster or discount guesses as to provenance offered by dealers or other knowledgeable friends. In some of our conclusions we differ, as is natural, with Dr. Chandra's expert attributions.

Thus, we like to think of the lady at her bath in no. 140 as Rādhā, lady love of Lord Kṛishṇa, with her attendant, being spied upon—as is frequently recorded in miniatures—by Kṛishṇa who, we feel, originally occupied the vanished third of the painting; and we feel that Rādhā's delightfully rounded small figure and the simple, Mandu-like architectural setting suggest Mewar as the source of the work.

With regard to no. 89, we think that the pinkish-red ground and simple, formal balance of plantains flanking the seated figure of Sarasvatī strongly suggest a seventeenth-century Bundi origin. Incidentally, Sarasvatī, goddess of learning and the arts, is very rarely pictured. Our only other painting of her is the rather brash Tanjore wooden panel from nineteenth- or twentieth-century South India (no. 269).

It is interesting to trace the passage of elements of style or composition from one court to another. The arched, flower-filled niches at the bottom of no. 143, which we think of as late seventeenth-century Mewāṛī, seem to have been taken from Malwa models such as no. 133. The rigid, formal pattern, even the green skin tone of the lady of the early Bundi no. 113 resemble other Malwa models (see Skira's *Painting of India*, page 69).

In the seventeenth century, Mewar, then a wild land of hills and lake-filled hollows ruled by proud Rāṇās who traced their heritage from the sun-god, was the most prolific source of paintings in all Rajputana (see nos. 87, 88, 90). The most popular subjects were those related to the romantic-religious Kṛishṇa tradition. As the eighteenth century rolled along, the emphasis shifted toward court scenes, influenced by the personal patronage of such rulers as Jagat Singh II, seen in nos. 93 and 94.

Rajput rulers, when they were not at war with one another or with the Mughals, gloried in the thrill of the hunt, and artists dutifully followed them into the field to record the kill (see no. 102). Mewar's hillsides are still dotted with shooting boxes and hunting lodges, but the tradition of hunt paintings flourished most productively at the rather late-established school of Kotah. In the late nineteenth century, Kotah artists were still turning out lively hunt scenes based, after a British fashion by then well established in India, on quick on-the-spot sketches (see nos. 127 and 128). It seems likely that hunt scenes like no. 97 and nos. 105 and 107 may be products of the Kotah nineteenth-century school (if possible compare no. 107 with sketches nos. 21 and 22 in Edwin Binney's *Rajput Miniatures* catalogue). We were especially intrigued by the animated sequence effect achieved in no. 107 by showing the same figures at several stages in the activity, moving from left to right—hunters, beaters and ill-fated tiger. (For different approaches to sequential painting, see nos. 210 and 250.)

To skip to very late, British-influenced paintings and sketches, however, is to miss the heart of the Rajput tradition. All through the eighteenth century many states of Rajputana continued to produce a large body of paintings, both religious and courtly. One of our favorite schools is that of Bundi, where our first two acquisitions (nos. 110 and 111) were produced between 1690 and 1710. The painters of Bundi created about legends and living rājās alike a fairytale world of glowing color, where pairs of birds courted in every tree and the sun-god sent his golden smile peeping over green hilltops, where every dwelling was a treasure-filled palace and each human being a figure of high romance (see nos. 114–119). It seems likely that some painters trained at the Mughal court (no. 114) and in Deccanī palaces (no. 121) worked in Bundi. The group of paintings known as "Bundi whites" to which no. 121 belongs reflect in an exaggerated way the Deccanī rulers' preference for ivory-white skins; from the Mughals came backgrounds opening to deep vistas and figures that move with a freedom rare in Rajput painting.

Late in the day of Bundi painting, craftsmen of nearby Kotah followed many of the Bundi models so closely that it is sometimes difficult to distinguish between work of the two neighboring states. Bundi miniatures, however, have in general a lightness, grace and delicacy, particularly in faces and figures, that those of Kotah do not match. Men of Kotah in the mid-nineteenth century did many sketches of Europeans and may well have produced the sketches in no. 108 as a step toward "Company School" work for the new British market. Surely it was a Bundi artist, though, who treated the fair-skinned, red-haired young gentleman seated on a gilt chair and sniffing a rose in no. 126 with such grace and courtesy. Surely Bundi produced the delightful, minute elephant taming scene in no. 129. And we think the lush fairy-tale illustration (no. 223) with its decadently elaborate ornamentation represents the end of the cycle at the court of Bundi, whose old palace suspended above the still waters of an artificial lake is in actuality fully as romantic a setting as any painter could fantasy.

The Bundi style had offshoots such as Kotah and, on a limited scale, Uniara—which may be represented by no. 114 or, as we were assured, by no. 135. Similarly, Mewar had stylistic offshoots such as the Kṛishṇa pilgrimage center of Nathdwara, where crude "bazaar-type" paintings of worship at the shrine are still produced for purchase as souvenirs even today. We acquired two, nos. 103 and 211, the latter a view of the celebration of Kṛishṇa's birthday with offerings at a secondary shrine of the great temple. Then we found a small scrap of an aerial view of the Nathdwara shrine (no. 104) done in the style of Jain iconography (see no. 6), so we added it.

Our interest in Nathdwara had been greatly enhanced by a visit, though the temple itself is closed to non-Hindus. Over a period of years we visited most of the sites of the local schools of painting. We did not succeed as well in exploring Marwari states as most others, regrettably since this western desert region includes three important centers of painting: Bikaner, Jodhpur and Kishangarh.

The painting of Bikaner is almost more Mughal than Rajput. For example, no. 32 seems completely Mughal and is indeed patterned after a Mughal painting (see Hambly's *Cities of Mughal India*, no. 97) but it was, we were assured, a product of Bikaner. The exquisite little lady in no. 174, dressed in her brocade trousers and sheer robe, is also quite Mughal. We were intrigued by comparisons between her and her twin in no. 175, evidently done, as was customary, from a common model sheet but probably a half-century later and with diminished sensitivity to textures and nuances and with the addition of a faintly discordant pool of silver water in the foreground.

The palette of Bikaner painters was generally more pastel—usually clear and bright but very gentle—than that of almost any other Indian school. Particularly good examples of this are nos. 176 and 177, and also, I think, no. 150, all three from *rāgamālā* sets inspired by musical modes. In addition, no. 150 with its minute glimpses of distant hills and palaces reminds us that in Bikaner more than at any other Rajput court painters picked up the Mughal interest in landscape and carried it to fanciful extremes, with ⅛ inch tall figures strolling on the terraces of meticulously detailed buildings which, one assumes, could be seen with utter clarity at such distances thanks to the clear, dry desert air of Bikaner.

Bikaner state was established by a scion of the Jodhpur royal family and the territories adjoin, so it is not surprising that painters of Jodhpur were influenced by work done at Bikaner. Probably the reverse was also true. Jodhpur's art, however, is in general much heavier, both in drawing and in color. Its classic facial style suggests self-indulgence and inordinate pride; its rājās preen themselves as they pose, lifting their full soft chins and staring off into the distance from bold, fish-shaped eyes. A few Jodhpur portraits are tendered with some of the delicacy of Bikaner (see no. 147) and the exquisite detail typical of the Mughals (see no. 151). It is also interesting to note at the base of no. 151 that the signature of the artist appears in infinitesimal but precise red lettering, a rarity among Hindu painters and Rajput paintings: "(work of) Sabi Bangari Gobind Ram Chitraki (painted by)." An occasional Jodhpur painting, like no. 145 or the flamboyant later court scene no. 154, also shows the Bikaner-Mughal influence in the very small distant scenes painted with consummate care. More typical perhaps of Jodhpur's prolific and slightly slapdash production are the zestful equestrian portrait (no. 152) and, in composition and figures if not in color, the night scene on a palace terrace, no. 183.

Much more reminiscent of Mewar, I should say, are nos. 143 and 149, while no. 144, with its ivory-skinned ladies and formal flower beds seems much more plausibly attributed to the Deccan; we were told that it came from the small Deccanī court of Kurnool.

Another state founded from Jodhpur was small Kishangarh. Like countless other areas it had long produced some folk art (see no. 171). In the second half of the eighteenth century, however, a brief and brilliant flowering of painting at Kishangarh was inspired by the Kṛishṇa-centered romance of Māhārajāh Sāvant Singh with a beautiful girl musician of his stepmother's retinue, called Bani Thani. The output of Kishangarh's royal studio was relatively small, the time span during which it did outstanding work was brief. The master painter Nihāl Chand developed, however, perhaps on the basis of actual likenesses, a model of female beauty so distinctive and arresting that it has made Kishangarh paintings much sought-after—and attractive to the talents of modern copyists. The dominant background influence was Mughal painting of the eighteenth-century court of Muhammad Shāh, with its long, slender, sveltely curved figures. We think of the long-legged beauty in no. 178 as epitomizing the type of late Mughal elegance that inspired the Kishangarh master, and fancifully imagine that she may even resemble Bani Thani, "The Lady of Fashion," in features. Similarly we like to think that the small portrait sketch, no. 162, may have been sat for by Māhārajāh Sāvant Singh himself.

Though classic Kishangarh paintings of the lavish type illustrated in the Dickinson-Khandala v ala *Kishangarh*

Painting, with their jewel-like small figures tucked into vast landscapes, were beyond our reach, we felt fortunate to be able to acquire several examples of the Kishangarh style as it developed—and soon declined. Thus the princess on the moonlit terrace among her maids (no. 158) exemplifies court painting in the years just preceding the catalytic Sāvant Singh–Bani Thani romance. Nos. 159 and 166 suggest that they may be fragmentary remnants of complex scenes of the high period of Kishangarh painting. No. 160, with its ladies pensively gathering fragrant grasses to take to the temple, is truly of the high period (and it is interesting to compare its background scene with those in Mughal no. 30 and Deccanī no. 42). The tinted drawing of Rādhā and Kṛishṇa (no. 163) epitomizes for us the tenderness of the Sāvant Singh-Bani Thani relationship. No. 167, though crudely done, has its own special claim to attention in that it shows, instead of Kṛishṇa and Rādhā, Vishṇu–Narayan and his consort Lakshmī on their customary lotus-pad throne, holding their several symbols in multiple (barely visible) hands. Kṛishṇa and Rādhā are never pictured with the four arms of gods and goddesses. Again the portrait of the little prince, no. 168, obviously the work of a scantily talented or careless craftsman, is intriguing for its very small inscription–dating, placing and ascribing the work. Together these two illustrate the decline of a once outstanding style.

Not far south of Kishangarh lies Ajmer, where Akbar built himself a small palace with a splendid adjoining mosque. Here tinted drawings were preferred to finished paintings, and a distinctive flavor was added to Mughal-style portraits and such other subjects as harem dancing girls and Kṛishṇa–Rādhā scenes (nos. 186–188).

The remaining major Rajput school of painting centered, not surprisingly, on the rich and powerful court of Amber state, which early in the eighteenth century moved to its new capital city of Jaipur. In our collection it seems likely that nos. 191 and 192 and perhaps also nos. 189 and 190 were painted at the fortress town of Amber before the move to the planned city on the plain. In their overall delicacy, in the drawing of the figures, and to some extent in the palette these are reminiscent of Bikaner paintings. This is not surprising, since the rulers of Amber and Bikaner became close allies of the Mughals during the sixteenth century while other Rajputs still held sternly aloof. Painting at Jaipur burgeoned during the eighteenth century and continued to flourish during much of the nineteenth century, though the output was more notable for quantity than quality. Painters were competent but rigid and uninspired, it seems, so that their work often has a wooden stiffness, as in nos. 195 and 196. In its latest period, Jaipur work often became rather garish, as in no. 199, or indulged in an exaggerated preciousness in scale (see no. 222).

Painting was naturally done at a number of minor centers near Jaipur as well as in the capital. The small princely state of Alwar, on the Jaipur–Delhi road, was the home of several able and prolific painters of the late eighteenth and nineteenth centuries; of them some carried the Mughal style to elaborately decorative extremes, as in nos. 48–50, while others pushed the Jaipur style into comparable excesses, similar to no. 199.

A more attractive—to me—offshoot of Jaipur painting is that of Malpura, a small commercial city of Jaipur state where paintings like nos. 194 and, I believe, 184 were done. The artists of Malpura, as in most other centers, developed their own distinctive facial models, in this instance based on an apple-shaped head with round cheeks and very low brow.

One additional school should be mentioned before moving northward to the Pahāṛī or Hill states. This is Bundelkhand, a Central Indian area bordering Gwalior state (where we believe no. 40 originated as a portrait of the ruler and his heir) and Bhopal (from which we believe no. 43 came). Bundelkhand, particularly the substate of Datia within it, produced in the late eighteenth century a large group of paintings readily recognizable from the filmy shawls worn as saris by the ladies and draped about the hips of the mutton-chop-moustached gentlemen, the feathery halos of new foliage surrounding trees and bushes, and a firm sense of composition based on strong diagonal lines of pure white palaces and pavilions and formal flower beds (see nos. 205–207). These three examples seem to us to be more than half a century later than nos. 202 and 203, which have a freshness and spontaneity lacking in the overly facile later paintings. Two other Bundelkhand paintings are nos. 209 and 210, in which the diagonal lines are particularly strong. It is interesting to compare these with Hill paintings such as no. 250. Since we bought no. 209, showing Rāma and his brother outside golden Laṅkā, from a dealer who said he had obtained it in a group from the Hills, it seems probable that a painter trained in Bundelkhand wandered northward and took up his occupation in the workshop of a Hill rājā, there to bring his own inbred characteristics to his newly adopted style.

The feudal states of the Pahāṛī or Hill region on the slopes of the Himalayas had had some folk painting for an indefinite time, but it was only at the end of the seventeenth century, when Aurangzeb's ban on the arts sent painters along with musicians fleeing from the imperial court, that the level of the strong, vibrant folk painting began to be raised to that of fine art.

The change came first to the western Hill states of Basohli and its neighbors, Mankot (see no. 233) and others. Here strong, simple portraits of Hill rājās such as nos. 226 and 227 came into fashion, along with *rāgamālā* sets distinguished from their contemporaries in Rajasthan by their deep, moody colors, a sense of energy, motion and emotion in their figures, and by such details as the frequent portrayal of bulging, hyperthyroid eyes and, on some of the women, jewelry embellished with bits of real, gleaming blue-green beetle wings (see nos. 228 and 230).

The Kṛishṇa legend soon became popular in the hills, and was pictured from the very first scene of the tale, in which Vishṇu and Lakshmī appear on their lotus pad throne (no. 229) to announce that Vishṇu will be born into the world of men as Kṛishṇa. (No. 167 is a late Rajput version of the same scene.) The legendary romance of the Muslim ruler Baz Bahadur of Malwa down in Central India and the Hindu lady Rupmati (who are seen at their initial meeting beside a bathing pool in no. 43) also took the fancy of Hill painters as they developed more sophistication from contact with Mughal masters and their work. The two lovers can be seen riding by moonlight, as they loved to do, in no. 225.

Bold coloring and generally simple, flat compositions and strongly drawn figures with thrusting profiles, all reminiscent of folk art, continued to dominate the painting of some courts longer than others. The trousered ladies chatting under the willow in no. 234 are folkish products of the eastern Hill state of Kulu in the mid-eighteenth century, but the vivid nos. 264 and 265 indicate that this folk style continued to be used far into the nineteenth century in the Kulu region.

By the mid-eighteenth century in most of the eastern Hill states a quite different approach to painting, much more strongly influenced by the elegance of late Mughal work with its emphasis on romantic and sybaritic elements in court life, had begun to develop. This is often, as in this catalogue, discussed under the blanket heading of Kangra Valley Style, though actually Kangra was only one central member of a large, sprawling family of mountain feudal states at which this general style was practiced with local variations. Admittedly it is difficult to be precise in assigning paintings to local sources. Not only did painters move from patron to patron and court to court; the paintings themselves were also presented as gifts to friends and neighbors, sent off with brides as part of their dowries, carried off by raiders in feudal wars, and otherwise removed from their points of origin to reappear much later in places where they caused confusion to scholars. Since we did become intrigued with the puzzle of local attributions, however, I might mention some of our guesses, backed by the opinions of dealers or expert friends.

To us no. 244, with its strong, simple color masses but slender, graceful figures for the couple on the terrace, suggests a link between earlier Hill styles and the lighter, gentler Kangra Valley idiom. It might well be called pre-Kangra. No. 232, with its poised and tranquil gentlemen seated on a simple terrace, presents a puzzle: it seems very like paintings identified as "Basohli–Bilaspur" in the Waldschmidts' *Miniatures of Musical Inspiration*, and also bears a strong resemblance to painting 76a in the Binney *Rajput Miniatures* catalogue identified as Nurpur. Our no. 258, which came to us at second-hand from Bilaspur, near the Punjab plains, is too late a work to be related easily to anything but the mid-nineteenth-century Sikh tradition. The pleasant drawing of the Kṛishṇa group, no. 237, and the group at the small golden Durga shrine in no. 238 as well as portraits nos. 240 and 242 we associate with Guler's gently composed style, with its straight-browed ladies, tranquil gentlemen and graceful flowering foliage. Nos. 252 and 259 we think may have been done at or near Guler later, when the fluid drawing of female figures had stiffened and the handling of foliage hardened. Embroideries such as nos. 266 and 267, picturing Kṛishṇa's dance with the cowmaids, the *Kṛishṇa Lila*, and the eight classic states of ladies in love, the *Nayika*, in colored thread rather than paint, are clearly from Chamba where this tradition flourished, but we also like to think of no. 253, showing Śiva and his family in their Himalayan home, as a Chamba painting. The lively hunt scene, no. 251, seems clearly to belong to the set identified by Khandalawala in his *Pahāṛī Painting* (no. 185) as a product of Mandi, where the gentle, sad-looking rājā of no. 231 once had ruled.

As to the work more directly associated with the Kangra area, we like to think that it is Rājā Sansar Chand of Kangra (1774–1823), prime patron of Kangra painting, who is shown worshiping Rāma and Sītā in no. 239, that it was Rājā Ranjit Dev of Jammu who posed for the Kangra-style portrait no. 241, while the dashing gentleman shown in no. 243 bears a strong resemblance to a known portrait of a leading Hill painter, Nainsukh.

In the nineteenth century the soft, warm coloring and tender, flowing line of Kangra Valley painting faded and hardened (see no. 254 for a pale, late example). The last vital change in the Hill styles came with the domination of the region by militant Sikhs from the Punjab plains. Their liking for sharp lines, intricate patterns and hard color is evidenced in portraits like nos. 261 and 262, romantic no. 255 with its canopy pattern reminiscent of the decoration of the Sikhs' Golden Temple at Amritsar, and by no. 258.

After the Sikhs came the period of British domination of painting as well as government in India. Painting done for the British is generally referred to, from its association with the East India Company, as Company School or Style. Under this heading are bulked the late products of several dying traditions of painting with mineral pigments on paper (see nos. 73, 74, and 80) as well as imitations of British quick sketches often tinted with watercolor washes (see nos. 75 of Bengal, 108 of Bundi–Kotah, 77 from the Deccan, 79 from the Punjab, 81 from Rajasthan and 82 from Mysore). In addition, some small scenes were done on mica (see no. 78 of Patna). Imitations of old paintings (nos. 57–59), daguerreotypes (no. 76 from Lucknow in Oudh), and palm-sized portraits on ovals of ivory in the western fashion were also produced.

It was probably daguerreotypes, ushering in the age of photography, that did a good deal to speed the final demise of the once vivid and enchanting tradition of Indian miniature painting.

Indian Painting

PRAMOD CHANDRA
University of Chicago

OF ANCIENT Indian painting, the only examples that have survived are the murals that decorate the interiors of a few temples, the most famous and extensive remains being found in the cave temples of Ajanta situated in the Deccan. The paintings here date from approximately the second half of the fifth century A.D., and it is therefore not surprising that, at their best, they show the same consummate qualities that unite spontaneously the physical and the spiritual—a characteristic of all Indian art of this period. Besides wall painting, there is literary evidence to show that work on a smaller scale was also done; however, nothing of this has survived.

Other than some very rare and fragmentary wall paintings at Sittanavasal and Badami which echo faintly (and in a local context) the traditions established during the fifth century, it is the manuscript illustrations produced in Eastern India which conserve elements of the ancient style. These show none of the radical changes that characterize the Western Indian style, the earliest examples of which are found on the walls of the temples at Ellora (eighth to tenth centuries A.D.). Paintings of the Eastern Indian school, the earliest discovered examples dating from the opening years of the eleventh century, are comparatively simple, with none of the expansive freedom of fifth-century work. This quality is displaced by an almost inhibited meticulousness. What the future held for this style is not known, for it came to an abrupt end two hundred years later with the Islamic invasions; the great centers of art from the Punjab to Bengal were laid waste and left in ruins. Thus, towards the end of the twelfth century, the iconoclastic and fanatical zeal with which the Muslim invaders persecuted the indigenous religions seems to have brought all artistic activities to a stop. The earliest Islamic monuments were built from the debris of temples, and it took some time before the arts began to flourish once again in a vastly changed environment.

This initial desolation did not prevail all over the country, and in Western India it seems to have done little to retard the growth of what is now called the Western Indian style. Besides the scanty paintings at Ellora and a few other temples, there are large numbers of manuscript illustrations now preserved primarily in the traditional Jaina libraries. They reveal an abstract and linear art, from which all traces of modeling have been gradually erased.

The compositions are strictly two-dimensional, and the drawing of the human figures are wiry and angular. The early paintings were done on palm-leaf folios, and the small rectangular panels are, in format, not unlike Eastern Indian paintings. The artists gradually became more ambitious, and in the fifteenth century, by which time paper had replaced palm leaf, the manuscripts became quite opulent and extravagant. Many were painted using the most costly materials. For the most part, however, all the wealth lavished and all the pious patronage extended did little to change the conservative mannerisms, and the style retained its strong individuality up to the end of the sixteenth century, paying little attention either to foreign styles, as those of Persia, or new styles that were beginning to develop indigenously.

The Muslim rulers, both of imperial Delhi and the provincial sultanates, once they had consolidated their power, appear to have patronized painting in addition to architecture. This is not so surprising, as some would have us believe for these rulers had before them examples of others in the Muslim world who paid scant attention to the injunctions of orthodox Islam in this regard. It was not the Western Indian style, however, that appealed to their taste, but traditions derived from the great Islamic styles abroad, notably those flourishing in Persia. Painters were probably imported from these countries, as were architects; illustrated manuscripts done there, being easily transportable, were certainly known. This activity gradually led to the development of what can correctly be called an Indo-Persian style, or styles, essentially based on the Persian manner, but affected to a greater or lesser extent by the new environment. Manuscript paintings done in India in this mixed manner are being increasingly discovered and recognized.

As stated earlier, normally the Western Indian style was steadfastly conservative, showing little inclination to change, or at least to change in any radical way. Now, however, we are able to see where this was not entirely the case. For example, from about the middle of the fifteenth century, we begin to get a few manuscripts which retain some of the mechanical mannerism of the Western Indian style, but which begin to show as well a more significant process of evolution. Thus, there developed by the sixteenth century a new and vigorous style, closely derived from the Western Indian style, but much more energetic and vital, deeply felt, and profoundly moving. The *Āranyaka Parva* of the *Mahābhārata*, dated A.D. 1516 (now in the Asiatic Society of Bombay), is the earliest of these manuscripts, closely followed by other paintings illustrating poetical romances, ballads, and Hindu legend. The isolation in which the Western Indian style had stubbornly dwelt now was also largely broken, and the new styles began to freely interact with each other.

This was the situation in Indian painting when the great Mughal dynasty established itself as the paramount power in Northern India. The Emperor Akbar, who came to the throne in 1556, was instrumental in giving what can only be called an entirely new direction to the history of Indian painting. Akbar established an atelier in which artists from various parts of India, belonging to the several traditions that were in existence at that time, were brought together. He put them under the initial superintendence of two Persian masters who had been invited to India by his father. Under the strong influence of his own individual and catholic taste, there evolved, in less than a lifetime, a style of the highest artistic achievement and of the greatest significance to the future development of other Indian schools. Naturalistic, refined, filled with vigorous movement and rich color, and vitally concerned with the reality of the every day world, the school of Akbar was followed by that of Jahāngīr (1605–1628), himself a connoisseur and a collector. Jahāngīr was particularly interested in portraiture, and studies of the greatest psychological perception, both of human beings, animals, birds, and flowers, were made by the great artists of the court. The movement of Akbari painting is stilled, the compositions are quieter, and line and color exquisitely refined and harmonious. In the reign of the Emperor Shāh Jahān (1629–1658), the easy and spontaneous sense of perception becomes inhibited, and the painting becomes hard and artificial, though yielding little to the Jahāngīr school in point of superb technique. There is a definite decline in quality of the work during the reign of the Emperor Aurangzeb (1659–1707), when the imperial atelier seems to have curtailed its activities. Few pictures in the high traditions of the previous reigns were made, and most of what is now available is definitely of inferior quality. The great days of Mughal painting were over, and though there was a brief revival during the reign of Muhammad Shāh (1719–1748), it was not long before the Mughal artist was confining his most accomplished work to the copying of older masterpieces.

During the eighteenth century, there came into being several local idioms of Mughal painting at various provincial courts which were becoming independent of the weakening Mughal power. But the work produced at these centers does not differ to any great extent from the style of Delhi.

During the nineteenth century, European influence began to be increasingly felt both in the provinces and at the center, ultimately leading to the formation of what is called the "Company Style." This impoverished and hybrid style fell into disuse about the early years of the twentieth century, when the modern period was ushered in by the School of Bengal, a combination of many tendencies including an attempted romantic revival of the past.

About the time the Mughal school was being nurtured at the court of Akbar, there was also emerging what is called the Rājasthānī style, which was a more direct continuation of the indigenous schools of the sixteenth century. It was for the most part but little affected by the naturalistic tendencies of the Mughal atelier. The subject matter is primarily legend and myth. Though there is little doubt that the Rājasthānī painter of the seventeenth century was acquainted with the Mughal style, this influence was often confined to the borrowing of superficial items such as dress and motif which hardly affected the nature of the style in any vital way. The Rājasthānī style was patronized at several centers, each with its own distinctive flavor. Some of these schools showed greater Mughal influence than others, but never with the disruption of the integrity of the style. Among the most important of the schools was that of Mewar which set the tone for much of Rajasthan. Bundi and later Kotah also became vital centers as did Marwar, Bikaner, Kishangarh, and Jaipur. There were probably many more, the history of some are only now being reconstructed.

The sharp contrast between the Mughal and Rājasthānī styles appears to have been much obscured during the eighteenth century, each influencing the other. The Rājasthānī schools, however, still preferred the abstract to the literal statement, and never abandoned their highly developed sense for strong and splendid color. Like the Western Indian style, the Rājasthānī style was also developed in areas outside Rajasthan, notably in Gujarat, Bundelkhand, and Malwa.

Allied to the early Rājasthānī style in spirit, content and technique were the products of the Pahāṛī style, the earliest examples of which probably date from slightly before or during the last quarter of the seventeenth century. The Basohli and related schools are reminiscent of early Rājasthānī painting, but we know little of their origins. Early Basohli painting, however, represents an art in confident possession of all its faculties and developed to the point of sophistication. Pahāṛī painting of the second half of the eighteenth century began to show evidences of pronounced Mughal influence, but was entirely successful in transforming the new elements into an essentially romantic and lyrical art.

The Deccan was the repository of a major art tradition of its own. In the sixteenth century and later, several schools of painting came into being at the courts of the various sultanates of the region. Their vision of the world was in some respects analogous to that of the Mughal court, but in addition there is to be seen a fresh poetic quality and freedom from the literal—perhaps due to the strength of surviving pre-Islamic traditions. The history of Deccanī painting broadly parallels that of Mughal painting with which it maintained close contact. The amount of work produced during the eighteenth century is very large and the quality fairly consistent. The abrupt decline visible in the Mughal school towards the end of the eighteenth century does not occur in the Deccan, where work extended into the nineteenth century only partially affected by the vogue for things European. The Deccan, however, could not escape the general decline of traditional schools over all of India at the time, and, with them was unable to outlast the century.

Eastern Indian Style

Among the earliest preserved manuscript paintings are those belonging to the Eastern Indian or the Pāla style as it is commonly called. The most important centers of this style appear to have been the great Buddhist monasteries of Bihar and Bengal. The paintings in this style were done on long palm-leaf strips and were usually of small size, being carefully and delicately executed unlike the rather free, cursive and pronouncedly angular work prevalent in Western India. In this respect, the miniatures are pictorial counterparts of Eastern Indian sculpture, adhering more conservatively to traditions established during the earlier Gupta and post-Gupta periods (fifth to seventh centuries A.D.). The style yields but grudgingly to the specifically medieval factor seen in the tense, angular contours and emphatic, linear distortions that are felt fairly early in Western and Central India. The Eastern Indian style appears to have come to an end with the conquest of the entire Gangetic plain by Islamic invaders towards the end of the twelfth century A.D.

1.

Folio from an unidentified Ms.
Eastern Indian Style, thirteenth century A.D.
$1\frac{5}{8} \times 16\frac{5}{8}$ inches

The fragment of a palm-leaf folio preserves two miniatures. To the left is an eight-armed male divinity carrying, among other objects, a bow and an arrow. The hand near the chest holds what appears to be a jar. To the right is a rectangular panel representing the Great Demise (*mahaparinirvāṇa*): the Buddha lying on a cot, leaning his head on the palm of the left hand.

Western Indian Style

The Western Indian style of painting seems to have come into being in Western India simultaneously with the medieval styles of sculpture and architecture. This was shortly after the collapse of the Gupta dynasty in Northern India and of the Vākāṭaka dynasty in Western India, during which time the caves of Ajanta were carved and painted. Among the earliest preserved examples of the Western Indian style are rare fragments surviving on the walls of the temples of Ellora, notably the magnificent Kailāsa (eighth century A.D.). Our fullest knowledge of the style, however, comes from the large number of illustrated manuscripts that have been preserved in the great traditional libraries of the Jaina communities of Gujarat and Rajasthan. The earliest of these, dating from about the eleventh century, are on palm leaf and follow the format of Eastern Indian miniatures, though more abstract and linear in concept. Palm leaf began to be discarded around the middle of the fourteenth century when it was replaced by paper. The style, partly because of the larger surface available for painting, becomes more elaborate and resplendent, no expense being spared in the use of costly gold and blue. It reaches its culmination in a magnificent *Kalpasūtra*, the major portion of which is in the Devaśā-nā-Pāḍā Library at Ahmedabad, one folio being in the Watson collection (Cat. no. 3). Not all manuscripts were equally sumptuous, and the prolific production seems to have made works of quality rare; but miniatures in the Western Indian style continued to be painted until the closing years of the sixteenth century. Thus, the style had a life span of about five hundred years, and throughout this period shows a remarkable unity and consistency. It was a conservative style, though this aspect is perhaps exaggerated by some scholars, chiefly on account of the "farther projecting eye" observed from the early years of its development to its end. Nevertheless, a careful study reveals that it did change and evolve, however subtly, often producing works of surprising intensity.

The Western Indian style flourished in Gujarat and Rajasthan, but was not confined to these regions. Examples have been found in Delhi, Mandu, and Jaunpur farther to the east, ranging in date from the fifteenth century and even earlier. There is reason to believe that after the disappearance of the Eastern

Indian style, the Western Indian style spread all over India, its impact being felt in Burma and South East Asia. It survives strongly up to the present day in the state of Orissa (Cat. no. 9).

2.

Folio from a Ms. of an
unidentified Sanskrit work
Western Indian Style (probably
Delhi), early fifteenth century
$4\frac{5}{8} \times 11\frac{1}{8}$ inches

Inset into the text are two rectangular panels. On the left, a king and queen conversing within a palace, outside of which stands a servant. On the right, two bearded men conversing in front of an antelope. Red ground.

The style is similar to a *Mahāpurāṇa* published by Moti Chandra, "An illustrated Ms. of the *Mahāpurāṇa* in the collection of Śrī Digambar Naya Mandir," *Lalit Kalā*, 5 (1959), pp. 68–81, and is dated by him to the close of the fifteenth century and assigned to Delhi. The discovery, by Mrs. Saryu Doshi of Bombay, of another manuscript with a colophon stating the date as A.D. 1404 and the provenance as Yoginīpura, confirms Dr. Moti Chandra's conjecture about the provenance, but suggests that the date has to be revised upwards.

3.

Folio from a *suvarṇākṣarī Kalpasūtra* Ms.
Western Indian Style, c. 1475
$4\frac{1}{4} \times 9\frac{7}{8}$ inches

The margins on the obverse are divided into several registers and filled with elaborate scenes. On the left, from top to bottom: two persons seated on thrones within a cusped arch outside of which are soldiers with swords and shields and a row of footmen preceded and followed by four-armed figures; a man on a swing rocked by two female attendants; a panel of musicians consisting of a drummer, trumpeter, *vīṇā* (lute) player and cymbalist; dancers performing before a figure holding a jar and seated on a stepped throne; and finally a man enthroned, wearing an *aṭpaṭī* turban with a slight projection at the back, and listening to four instrumentalists wearing similar turbans. The right margin is also divided into registers: a cusped arch with figures attended by swordsmen; a royal figure on a throne with attendants, all in worshipful gestures, seated around a *sthāpanā*; musicians, a lady reclining on a couch with attendants in service; and a wrestling performance.

The text, in gold letters (*suvarṇākṣarī*) on a ground of blue, has narrow panels on the top and bottom showing dancers performing to music before a figure seated on a swing and horses led by grooms, each groom wearing a flat turban from which flutter bands of cloth that may be the turban ends.

The main illustration, in contrast to the lively movement and color of the margins, is in a strictly hieratic tradition, painted predominantly in blue, red and gold; it shows a four-armed divinity applying a *tilaka* mark on the forehead of a man seated on a throne.

The reverse of the folio is not as elaborate, showing female figures in dance postures in the left and right margins. The text is bordered on the top and bottom by floral meanders.

It is remarkable that in spite of the variety of the subject matter represented—in sharp contrast to what we are generally accustomed to in Western Indian painting—the style of the margins and of the main illustration is identical. Thus, this manuscript emphasizes the conservative aspects of the style, in contrast to the Jaunpur manuscript of 1465, and more so the Mandu *Kalpasūtra* of 1439 and the *Kālakāchārya-kathā* of the same provenance and of about the same date, where the style itself is beginning to show definite signs of change. The Devaśā-nā-pāḍā manuscript is thus among the final and great achievements of the Western Indian style, while the Jaunpur and Mandu manuscripts illustrate a movement that flowers into a new style in the succeeding years.

The folio, numbered 129, definitely belongs to the splendid manuscript of the *Kalpasūtra* and *Kālakāchārya-kathā* in the Jaina library situated in the Devaśā-nā-pāḍā, Ahmedabad. Forty-three folios are known to be missing from that manuscript, and this is one of them. It was formerly in the collection of Mr. Sarabhai Nawab, Ahmedabad; and is reproduced in Moti Chandra, *Jaina Miniature Painting*, Fig. 138b.

REFERENCES:

WILLIAM NORMAN BROWN, "A Jaina Manuscript from Gujarat illustrated in Early Western Indian and Persian styles," *Ars Islamica*, IV (1937), pp. 154–75.

MOTI CHANDRA, *Jaina Miniature Painting from Western India*, Ahmedabad, 1949, p. 39.

KARL KHANDALAVALA and MOTI CHANDRA, *New Documents of Indian Painting*, Bombay, 1970, pp. 29–40.

3

PRAMOD CHANDRA, "A Unique *Kālakācharya Kathā* Ms. in the style of the Mandu *Kalpasūtra*," *Bulletin of the American Academy of Benares*, No. 1 (1967), pp. 1–10.

MOTI CHANDRA and KARL KHANDALAVALA, "An illustrated *Kalpasūtra* painted at Jaunpur in A.D. 1465," *Lalit Kalā*, 12 (1962), pp. 9–15.

MOTI CHANDRA and KARL KHANDALAVALA, "A consideration of an illustrated manuscript from Mandu dated 1439," *Lalit Kalā*, 6 (1959), pp. 8–29.

4.

The transfer of the embryo:
folio from a Ms. of the *Kalpasūtra*
Western Indian Style,
late fifteenth century
$4\frac{5}{8} \times 11\frac{3}{4}$ inches

Triśalā, the queen, reclines on a bed, her head turned away from the goat-headed Harinegameshin, who holds the embryo in his hand.

5.

Kālaka preaching to the Sāhī king:
folio from a Ms. of the
Kālakāchārya-kathā
Western Indian Style,
late fifteenth century
$4\frac{1}{4} \times 10\frac{3}{8}$ inches

The Sāhī king, dressed in the Muslim fashion, holds a sword across the shoulder. He is addressed by the monk Kālaka, dressed in a spotted white garment. Lions and a drummer in the lower register.

The face of the king, shown in two-thirds profile, in contrast with other faces which are shown either in profile or in full view, is inspired by contemporary Islamic painting conventions.

6.

Saṁvasaraṇa of a Tīrthaṅkara:
folio from a Ms. of the *Kalpasūtra*
Western Indian Style,
late fifteenth century
$4\frac{5}{8} \times 3\frac{3}{4}$ inches

The Tīrthaṅkara, crowned, is seated in the center of a series of circular enclosures atop a mountain. In the corners are various animals and birds.

Orissan Style

The region of Orissa, on the eastern seacoast, preserves the traditions of the Western Indian style right up to modern times. Miniature paintings in the form of book illustrations are found beginning in the seventeenth century, though the major portion of surviving materials dates from the eighteenth and nineteenth centuries. Even at this date, when palm-leaf manuscripts had largely disappeared from most parts of India, the Orissan artist and scribe continued to use it as a favored medium. Paintings on cloth, related to the temple of Puri and its cult, continue to be produced in large numbers for the pilgrim trade even today.

7.

Illustration from
an unidentified Ms.
Orissa, eighteenth century
$2 \times 16\frac{1}{4}$ inches

Obverse: In the large panel to the left is a court scene. The person seated opposite the king turns around to speak to an attendant. In the next panel is an attendant addressing what appears to be a group of entertainers. These consist of a saluting figure garbed like an ascetic, a drummer, an acrobat carrying rings and a staff, and a woman. The small panel at the extreme left is decorated with trees and a river with fishes; the panel on the left contains a boat on a river.

Reverse: A king is shown with an ascetic who has turned around to look out of the room. Behind the servant carrying the fan are two seated figures, who cover their eyes with their hands. In the panel to the right, is the same group as on the obverse; the person at their head raises his hands in a vigorous gesture, as though pronouncing a curse.

7

8.

Devī slaying the Buffalo-demon
Orissa, eighteenth or nineteenth century
$4\frac{7}{8} \times 7\frac{1}{2}$ inches

The four-armed Goddess, carrying the conch and discus, attributes usually associated with Vishṇu, pierces the demon with the trident. He has just emerged from the body of the buffalo, whose head has been severed from the body. Two female attendants, one on each side, wave fly whisks.

The building in which the action takes place is in the shape of a temple with horizontal roof tiers and an *āmalasāraka* on top. Outside the temple are ascetics, hands raised in adoration.

The painting is a fragment, spreading across several strips of palm leaves which have been strung together. Only three of these have survived.

9.

A Jagannātha *paṭ*
Orissa, twentieth century
$7\frac{1}{8} \times 6\frac{1}{2}$ inches

In the center of the large temple are shown the images of Jagannātha, Subhadrā, and Balarāma attended by worshippers. Various mythological scenes are cursively painted in the several registers. These include: on top, the ten incarnations of Vishṇu; in the second register, to the left, the well-known episode of Balarāma and Kṛishṇa meeting the milkmaid Manikā as they advance, incognito, ahead of the Orissan expedition to Kāñchī, and to the right, the battle of Rāma with Rāvaṇa. In the lowest register are depicted chariots of the divinities and the Lion Gate (*siṁhadvāra*) of the temple.

Indo-Persian Style

Very little is known about painting in India which must have been patronized by the new Muslim rulers and their courts from the early years of the Islamic conquest in the twelfth century A.D. to the rise of the Mughal school under the great Emperor Akbar (1556–1605). It was supposed by some that there was simply no such painting, notwithstanding the numerous literary references and the well-established tradition of ignoring the strict injunctions of Islam in this matter in other Islamic lands—notably in Persia (with which India had the closest contacts) and in the neighboring kingdom of Ghazni. More recently the belief that there was no Islamic painting has been changing, largely due to the works of scholars of Islamic and, particularly, of Persian painting; these scholars have noticed the strong non-Persian features of several miniatures that were previously regarded as Persian, however uncomfortably. Additionally, a few manuscripts (done in a more or less superficial Persian manner, but avowedly painted at Indian courts) have come to light which clearly reveal the existence in India of a style that can only be called "Indo-Persian." Works in this Indo-Persian style were usually inspired by the various regional idioms existing in Persia; they are sometimes so close to their origins that they can only be regarded as provincial Persian schools. Very often, however, they possess a distinct sense of color and line which makes them as truly Indian as those contemporary works of architecture built by Islamic invaders.

REFERENCES:

SIMON DIGBY, "The literary evidence for painting in the Delhi Sultanate," *Bulletin of the American Academy of Benares*, No. 1 (1967), pp. 47–60.

R. ETTINGHAUSEN, *Paintings of the Sultans and Emperors of India*, (New Delhi, 1961); "The Bustan Manuscript of Nāṣir Shāh Khaljī," *Mārg*, XII (1959), pp. 42–43.

ROBERT SKELTON, "The Ni'mat Nāmah: a Landmark in Malwa Painting," *Mārg*, XII (1959), pp. 44–50.

10.

Tā'īr being put to death:
folio from an illustrated Ms. of
the *Shāh-nāma*
Indo-Persian Style,
early sixteenth century
$8\frac{7}{8} \times 6\frac{1}{8}$ inches

A king, seated on a throne, watches a prisoner being hacked apart with a saw. Courtiers watch the gruesome scene. The background is filled with light tufts of grass and a few flowering plants, two of them seen in horizontal cross section. The edges of the mound which form the horizon line are marked with dots. Ornamental clouds in the sky, a river in the foreground.

The painting is reminiscent of the *Ni'mat-nāma* done for Nāṣir Shāh Khaljī at Mandu, c. 1502, and may have been painted in Malwa. It is derived from the Turkoman style of Shiraz, and would appear to be closer to its source than the *Ni'mat-nāma*, which shows marked Indian features. Cf. Robert Skelton, "The Ni'mat Nāmah: a Landmark in Malwa Painting," *Mārg*, XII (1959), Col. Pl. A.

10

11.

A man with a camel
Indo-Persian Style,
mid-sixteenth century
$4\frac{1}{8} \times 5\frac{7}{8}$ inches

A man attempts to mount a camel, having seized it by the legs. Beyond a stream, with water done in a "basket pattern," are undulating rocks behind which are groups of figures peeping at the scene.

The painting shows several Persian features, but the coloring indicates an Indian origin.

12.

A prince and a princess
Indo-Persian Style,
mid-sixteenth century
$5\frac{1}{4} \times 5\frac{1}{8}$ inches

The prince, backed by an orange bolster, is seated on a light green carpet. A tray, a jar and two burning candlesticks are laid out on the floor around him. The princess, who enters drawing aside the curtain, looks at an old woman who has flung herself at her feet.

The coloring is strongly reminiscent of paintings related to those of the Prince of Wales Museum *Chandāyan*, most notably in the mauve background with floral design and the strong yellows. Cf. Karl Khandalavala and Moti Chandra, *New Documents of Indian Painting*, Figs. 156–75.

12

Mughal Style

A revolution takes place in the history of Indian painting during the reign of the Emperor Akbar (1556–1605), easily the most outstanding king of the Mughal dynasty and one of the greatest rulers of India. As a boy, he learned painting under Khwāja 'Abdu'ṣ Ṣamad, a Persian painter employed by his father Humāyūn. When he came to the throne, he organised an extremely strong and vigorous atelier at the court where artists from all over India were employed, together with a sprinkling of foreign masters versed in the Persian styles. Under the patronage of Akbar and the influence of his individual taste, a new school came into being which drastically transformed the various disparate traditions that existed in India at that time. This process is clearly visible in the unique *Tūṭi-nāma* of the Cleveland Museum of Art. The ambitious *Dāstān-i-Amīr Hamzah* (the largest surviving portion of which is now housed in the Museum für Angewandte Kunst, Vienna) shows a more evolved style full of the most vigorous and dynamic movement, bold color, and a sure perception of the reality and decorative beauty of the living world. This early energetic phase continued until c. 1580, when a number of historical manuscripts were illustrated. With these, books of fables, poetical manuscripts, and copies of the Persian and Hindu epics were made. With the passing of time, the early vigor gave way to a studied refinement, accompanied by brush work of the most delicate virtuosity—a phase which reached its culmination around the close of the sixteenth century. With Jahāngīr (1605–1628), taste turned away from book illustrations to primarily portraiture of human beings and animals. The brilliance of earlier coloring is subdued, the movement quieter and more solemn. Shāh Jahān seems to have paid more attention to architecture, though he was also fond of painting, as is witnessed by the *Shāh Jahān-nāma* (in the Windsor Castle Library) and the magnificent albums that were brought together by his orders. Work during his reign lacks the fresh life that is visible below the surface of work of the Jahāngīr period; the portraits are really more like effigies. The colors are meticulously finished, possessing the brilliance of enamel.

Mughal painting seems to have declined rapidly after Shāh Jahān, very little work of quality surviving from the reign of Aurangzeb. In the early eighteenth century, during the reign of Muhammad Shāh (1719–1748), there seems to have been a brief revival which does not appear to have lasted too long. Aside from the king and the court, a large number of genre scenes depicting ladies on terraces, the various emotional states of lover and beloved, musical parties, carousels, etc. became quite popular. A great deal of the work of this type has survived, some of it endowed with an obtuse romantic quality.

Mughal painting came to an end during the reign of Shāh Ālam (1759–1806), when the empire ultimately shrank to the area enclosed by the walls of the Red Fort at Delhi. The artists of the court seem to have mainly occupied themselves by turning out copies of old masterpieces in the Imperial Library. Heavy with color and leaden in appearance as much of this work is, we occasionally get a fine hand that seems to touch fleetingly the source of real life.

Aside from the imperial capital, the Mughal style was cultivated in the new centers of power that were growing up in the provinces. Among the more important were those at Lucknow and

Murshidabad, where prosperous and powerful kingdoms had grown up owing only the most nominal allegiance to the central power.

During the eighteenth century, much of the work was produced in ateliers that catered to other needs and tastes than those of kingly patrons. This popularization of the Mughal style was a process also known earlier. We get miniatures which are obviously the work of painters employed outside the imperial atelier from at least the early years of the seventeenth century. Their work gives expression to the generally simpler and bolder traditions of the indigenous styles (so drastically transformed in the imperial atelier) which once again come to the surface. The Mughal style, through these works and other ways exercized a profound influence, generally beneficent, on the other Indian schools of this period. In turn, particularly from the last quarter of the seventeenth century onwards, the Mughal style was itself subject to their influence, often receiving from them a fresh interest in the romantic and the colorful.

REFERENCES:

S. C. WELCH, *The Art of Mughal India*, (New York, 1964).

I. STCHOUKINE, *La Peinture Indienne*, (Paris, 1926).

PERCY BROWN, *Indian Painting under the Mughals*, (Oxford, 1924).

13.

A tree watered by human blood: miniature from an unidentified Ms.
Mughal Style, c. 1575
$7 \times 5\frac{5}{8}$ inches

A man directs a servant to pour blood from a large bowl into the roots of a tree that bears human heads as fruits. The body of a man with the head severed, which apparently provided the blood for the tree, lies on the ground. He is bewailed by a lady with unbraided hair who throws her hands up in anguish. Around are numerous figures, most of them in gestures expressing astonishment or bewilderment. In the foreground are men on horseback, amazed at the sight.

The bright color, vigorous gestures, and the softly painted rock and tree forms make this painting contemporary with or a little earlier than the British Museum *Dārāb-nāma*. The *Ḥamzah* tradition is present, but this painting is later than that work.

13

14.

The birth of a prince
Mughal Style, c. 1605
9×6⅜ inches

A woman lies on a canopied and curtained bed placed in a palace room. She is attended by women wearing tall Chāghtāi caps, one of whom is seated near the bed with the new baby cradled in her arms. To the left is a king on a throne, wearing a turban with a *kūlah* of the type worn by the Emperor Humāyūn. The news of a son's birth is brought to him by a courtier who raises his hands in salute. Beyond the walls are trees with tops of the foliage visible and a sky with clouds.

The picture is extensively retouched and repainted, notably the sky, the parapet and terrace, and the red canopy and curtains of the bed.

15.

A prince restraining an elephant
Mughal Style, c. 1615
7×10 inches

A prince, seated on an elephant, attempts to restrain the creature with a goad. A horseman, who has moved ahead of the elephant, turns around to face the unruly beast. Behind the elephant is a retainer carrying a staff to which is attached a firewheel; while yet another retainer races ahead with a similar object in hand.

The painting has a strong "popular Mughal" flavor, particularly in the flat yellow expanse of the background and the rather stiff manner in which the limbs and head are joined to the body.

15

16.

Folio from a Ms. of the romance of Mādhavānala and Kāmakandalā
Mughal Style, c. 1605
$6 \times 6\frac{1}{2}$ inches

Obverse: A man wearing a *dhotī* (lower garment), *dupaṭṭā* (scarf), and a turban is lying on a bed, at the foot of which are two women conversing, and at the head of which is a partly preserved figure of a seated woman. Red background with white curtains on top.

Reverse: A man dressed in a bright red *dhotī* lifts a child from the bushes where he has been abandoned. A river in the foreground, light blue sky above a curving horizon. The top portion of the folio is taken up by seven lines of text.

The painting is supposed to belong to a series dated A.D. 1603. The date could be correct. The work is definitely of the Popular Mughal school, and is in all probability the work of Ustād Sālivāhana. For a later work by the same artist see Pramod Chandra, "Ustād Sālivāhana and the development of a popular Mughal art," *Lalit Kalā*, 8 (1960), pp. 25–46.

The romance appears to have been popular, another series being illustrated in K. Khandalavala, M. Chandra and

16

16

P. Chandra, *Miniature Paintings from the Śrī Motichand Khajanchi Collection*, New Delhi, 1960, p. 27, no. 17.

17-18.

Two folios from a Ms. illustrating the story of Yūsuf-Zulaykhā
Mughal Style, c. 1610
$4\frac{1}{2} \times 2\frac{3}{4}$ inches

(17.) A princess, seated in a terrace pavilion, converses with a man standing below. The walls of the building are painted with large floral shrubs similar to those behind the mauve wall. In the foreground is a groom attending a horse and conversing with the doorkeeper.

(18.) Zulaykhā, in deep thought, leans forward resting her hands on her knees. Facing her is an attendant, bowing respectfully. The yellow ground in front of the pavilion is liberally sprinkled with stylized floral plants, which also decorate the walls of the house.

The large patches of color, flat composition, and the consciously decorative use of floral design, clearly indicate that the paintings belong to the Popular Mughal school. They are reminiscent of the splendid folio of the *Gīta Govinda* in the Cowasji Jehangir Collection (K. Khandalavala and M. Chandra, *Miniatures and Sculptures from the collection of the late Sir Cowasji Jehangir, Bart.*, Bombay, 1965, no. 16, p. 17) and are of approximately the same date. Paintings of this type must have played a strong part in the development of the Rājasthānī schools, particularly the style of Mewar associated with Sāhabadī (cf. the *Khajanchi Catalogue*, no. 23, and figs. 29 and 30).

18

19.

A woman visiting an ascetic
Mughal Style, c. 1605–1610
$5\frac{3}{4} \times 3\frac{3}{4}$ inches

A lady dressed in a yellow *chākdār jāmā* (tunic), the points of which almost reach the ground, stands respectfully before a dervish and offers him a box on a tray. Craggy rocks in the background and the foreground.

Though the work of a lesser hand, the style of the miniature follows that of the painters of the *Anwār-i-Suhailī* in the British Museum. There are signs of repair and some retouching, but the picture as a whole is of the early Jahāngīr period. Cf. J.V.S. Wilkinson, *The Lights of Canopus*, London, n.d.

20.

The hoopoe
Mughal Style, c. 1610
$8\frac{5}{8} \times 7$ inches

The bird is painted against a background of pink rocks, a gold sky, and a maple tree with sinuous trunk. The gold appears to have been repainted and the under-drawing of what could have been an earlier study or version is visible in some places, particularly beneath the rocks in front of the bird's chest.

The brushwork is delicate; but the contours of the bird are a little stiff. The composition follows traditions of animal painting set up in the reign of Akbar (cf. E. Kühnel and H. Goetz, *Indische Buchmalereien*, Berlin, 1924, Pl. 10), but the somewhat subdued and thin outlines of the rocks establish it to be a work of the Jahāngīr period. It is reminiscent of a study of a bird by Abūl Ḥasan now in The Metropolitan Museum of Art, New York (no. 55.121–10–15). The arabesque strips pasted at the top and bottom are of good quality and would appear to be of a date approximately contemporary to the main painting.

21.

Portrait of a dervish
Mughal Style, second quarter of the seventeenth century
$2 \times 1\frac{5}{8}$ inches

The man is shown in a pensive mood, left hand raised to the cheek. Both the shoulders are covered by a robe, one end of which he holds in his right hand.

The drawing is meticulous and detailed, but lacks the soft sensuousness of most work of the Jahāngīr period. The outline and the rhythm is comparatively hard and emphatic suggesting the closing years of Jahāngīr's reign or the early years of the reign of Shāh Jahān to be the period of production.

22.

A noble and a holy man
Mughal Style, mid-seventeenth century
$6\frac{1}{4} \times 3\frac{1}{2}$ inches

The noble has dropped his bow and raises his hand in astonishment at the appearance of the holy man. Two wild men, one of them flourishing a club, the other apparently hurling a stone and struggling with a soldier, are shown in the hilly landscape. The drawing is accented with touches of color.

23.

Capturing wild elephants
Mughal Style,
late seventeenth century
$10\frac{1}{4} \times 6\frac{3}{4}$ inches

In the foreground is a herd of elephants frolicking by the hilly banks of a lake or a river. Immediately behind, an elephant of the herd struggles with a tame elephant which attempts to subdue it. One of the wild elephant's legs has been lassoed, the other end of the rope forming a noose around the leg of a small elephant in the foreground. Galloping horseman and other elephant hunters in the background.

24.

A lady with a wine cup
Mughal Style,
late seventeenth century
$5\frac{1}{8} \times 3$ inches

The lady holds a basket against her hip with her left hand; a wine cup is implausibly perched on her right hand. Chartreuse ground.

The picture is an adaptation of a European engraving or painting, and is in the tradition of "curiosities" known as early as the reign of Akbar. Often several features of the original were not clearly understood, resulting in anomolies like the precariously located wine cup and the curious manner of holding the basket.

20

21

25.

The Emperor Jahāngīr
holding a globe
Mughal Style,
late eighteenth century
$8\frac{7}{8} \times 6\frac{3}{8}$ inches

The emperor, with nimbus, is symbolically attired. He wears an elaborately plumed helmet, a richly embroidered coat with curious stiff pleats projecting behind the neck and over the shoulder, and tall riding boots. A shield is slung over his shoulder; a sword hangs horizontally from a baldric which dangles from the waist. The globe is decorated with lions and deer, in peaceful coexistence; above the globe is the imperial seal with the names of Timūr and his descendants; crowning the seal is the Timūrid crown. In the background, amidst a hilly landscape, is the imperial army on the march.

The Persian inscription in four lines on the top right purportedly dates to the day of Nauroz in the thirteenth regnal year of Jahāngīr and refers to the victorious Mughal army. The painting is a copy of the fine picture in the Freer Gallery of Art done by Abūl Ḥasan, Jahāngīr's favorite painter, which lacks, however, this inscription.

25

26.

Geese near a stream
Mughal Style, probably late seventeenth century
$7\frac{1}{2} \times 4\frac{1}{2}$ inches

In the foreground are four animated geese, their heads clustered together. Above them are another pair of geese flapping their wings and three more in states of motion and rest. The tinted ground is covered with stylized floral plants.

The drawing appears to be inspired by a work of the Jahāngīr period. The calligraphic line lacks fluency, and at times is hesitant and faltering; but it does not possess the rigidity of eighteenth-century work.

27.

A hunter trapping deer
Mughal Style, probably late seventeenth century
$5\frac{3}{4} \times 5\frac{5}{8}$ inches

A man riding on a chocolate-colored horse leans forward in an attempt to snare a fleeing black buck in his outstretched bow. Rocky mounds with trees in the background; a lake in the foreground.

The picture is an attempt to imitate a work of the late Jahāngīr period in the handling of landscape elements, particularly the trees with fluffy bluish foliage growing out of conical mounds at the base of the trunk. In this case, however, the color is inky and dull and the line lacks clarity, particularly in the figure of the horseman, raising the possibility of the picture being a later copy.

28.

Portrait of Shāh Jahān
Mughal Style, c. 1700 or later
$7\frac{5}{8} \times 4\frac{1}{8}$ inches

The emperor, with nimbus and wearing a chartreuse *jāmā*, holds a sword which rests across his shoulder and a fly whisk. The graying beard suggests advanced age. The stiff posture and line are characteristic of Mughal painting in the eighteenth century.

29.

Portrait of a nobleman
Mughal Style,
late eighteenth century
$8\frac{1}{2} \times 4\frac{3}{4}$ inches

The nobleman, standing, holds his hands in a gesture of respect. Apple-green ground.

The painting, which is carefully finished, is an attempt at imitating the style of portraiture current late in the reign of Jahāngīr and Shāh Jahān. The flesh tones, however, are yellow rather than pink, the jewels lack luminosity, the pleats of cloth at the wrist lack volume, and the dark black shield with six gilt knobs placed off balance introduces a discordant element—all suggesting a style characteristic of the reign of Shāh Ālam. A large number of copies of earlier Mughal works were made at this time, some of good quality like the present example, and some in a much more garish and vulgar manner (see Cat. no. 48).

30.

Aurangzeb crossing a lake in a boat
Mughal Style, c. 1700
$7\frac{1}{8} \times 11\frac{3}{4}$ inches

The aged emperor, enthroned, sits in the front of the boat, his head bent over a book. Behind him are four standing courtiers, the first with a hawk perched on his hand indicating that the party may be setting out on a hunt. Several men ply the oars. Among the other seated figures is a man holding a musket. In the background are hills, a walled city, and troops in procession.

The miniature is in a bad state of preservation, and some portions are retouched, notably the water and a few of the seated figures in the boat.

30

31.

Princes in conversation
by a riverside
Mughal Style, early
eighteenth century
$6\frac{1}{4} \times 3\frac{1}{2}$ inches

The young men are seated on a carpet, partaking of food and drink spread before them in cups and on trays. In the foreground is a pool of water banked with a thick growth of flowering plants. In the background is a river with swimming women, and, on the farther shore, rows of dark trees and a mosque.

The upper portion of the picture, including the river and the swimming women, appears to be a later and less-accomplished addition.

32.

Rāginī Rāmakarī
Mughal Style, early
eighteenth century
$7\frac{1}{4} \times 4\frac{1}{4}$ inches

A lady, seated on a bed, draws away from her lover who falls at her feet. A room with gray walls and a bright orange curtain in the background. Cf. Cat. no. 181.

32

For an earlier Mughal version of the picture see Stchoukine, *La Peinture Indienne*, Pl. LVI.

33.

Women worshipping Śiva Liṅga
Mughal Style, period of
Muhammad Shāh (1719–1748)
$5\frac{1}{2} \times 4\frac{1}{8}$ inches

Within an illuminated shrine beneath the shadow of a tree is placed an altar with a Liṅga. A lady with long matted locks of hair makes offerings to the image, while behind are two more figures in easy and contemplative postures.

The crescent moon and clouds and the gray tones of color suggest that it is night.

34.

A *yoginī*
Mughal Style, period of
Muhammad Shāh (1719–1748)
$5\frac{3}{8} \times 3\frac{1}{2}$ inches

A *yoginī*, holding a peacock-feather whisk in one hand and a long trident in the other, stands against a dusty ground and sky. Her hair is coiled in a bun at the back of the head.

35.

A lady dressing her hair
Mughal Style,
mid-eighteenth century
$5\frac{3}{8} \times 2\frac{7}{8}$ inches

The lady has loosely wrapped a *dhotī* around her waist and is busy coiling her hair into a bun. The torso is bare except for numerous necklaces.

36.

Ladies drinking
on a terrace
Mughal Style,
mid-eighteenth century
$9\frac{1}{4} \times 6\frac{5}{8}$ inches

The women are seated on a terrace by the riverside. They are attended by fly-whisk bearers and musicians.

37.

Portrait of a nobleman
Mughal Style (Murshidabad),
c. 1760
$12\frac{3}{4} \times 10\frac{1}{8}$ inches

The nobleman, rose in hand, reclines against a bolster and listens to a singer accompanied by two musicians, one playing a drum, the other tuning a stringed instrument. The scene is laid on a garden platform fenced off by a low railing, on both sides of which are stylized beds of roses.

Cf. R.S. Skelton, "Murshidabad Painting," *Mārg*, x (December, 1956), p. 16, fig. 10.

37

38.

A love scene
Mughal Style (probably Lucknow), mid-eighteenth century
$7 \times 4\frac{3}{8}$ inches

A man, seated on a carpet, embraces his beloved who shyly turns away. The evening hour is indicated by the gray tones of the walls and the burning candles. Elaborate architectural setting.

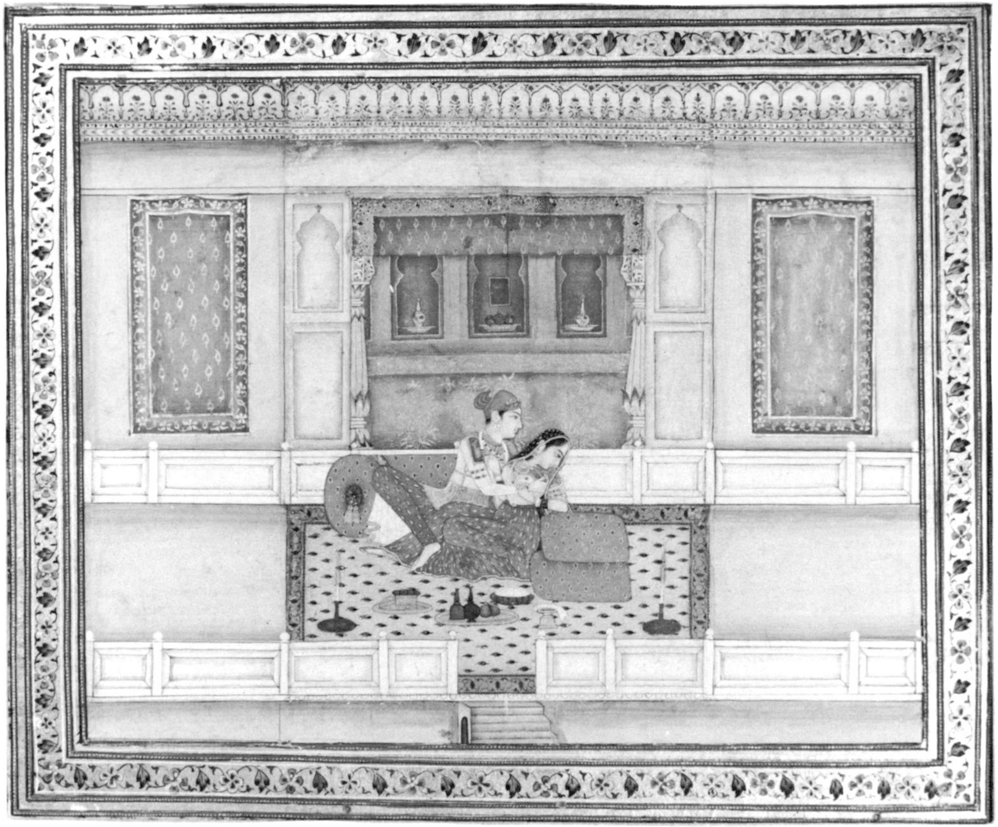

38

39.

Musicians on a terrace
Mughal Style (probably Lucknow),
mid-eighteenth century
$8\frac{7}{8} \times 6\frac{5}{8}$ inches

A lady, lavishly bejewelled, sits on a terrace next to a bed. She holds the stem of a *hukkā* pipe in one hand and a *tānpūrā* in the other. Facing her is a woman playing on a *tablā*, and behind her is yet another woman animatedly gesturing with her fingers in response to the music. An attendant holding a bottle of wine leans drowsily against the bed.

Gray night sky with a silver moon. Dark and richly painted groves of plantains and other trees on the sides. A fountain and flower beds in the foreground.

The Persian inscription on the reverse identifies the lady as "Roshanābādī, an inmate of the harem of Muhammad Shāh." The price of the painting is stated to be Rs. 325 and the painter is identified as Honhār. This Honhār, if the inscription is reliable and not a later addition, is obviously a different person than his famous namesake who belonged to the atelier of Shāh Jahān.

39

40.

Nobleman with child on a terrace
Mughal Style (probably Lucknow), mid-eighteenth century
$7 \times 4\frac{3}{4}$ inches

A nobleman, with scarf painted in striking yellow, smokes a *hukkā*. Standing next to him is a child wearing a close-fitting cap. Bright sky with white and red clouds.

A seal on the reverse indicates that the picture was formerly in the collection of Purushottam Mawji.

41.

Princess with attendants in a palace
Mughal Style (probably Lucknow), late eighteenth century
Colored stencil
$15\frac{3}{4} \times 9\frac{1}{2}$ inches

A princess is shown in the foreground to the right. Behind her stretch away the various buildings, pavilions, and gardens of a royal establishment.

The drawing appears to be half of a full composition, the right half being missing. The surface has been pricked with holes to allow for making tracings.

Receding vistas of this type, clearly influenced by European ideas of perspective, become increasingly popular from the eighteenth century onwards, particularly at Lucknow.

42.

A palace scene
Mughal Style (probably Lucknow), late eighteenth century
$10\frac{3}{4} \times 8\frac{3}{4}$ inches

On opposite sides of a patio garden are to be seen a lady with attendants and her musicians. Figures are also shown seated on the several terraces of the buildings. Beyond, on the banks of an artificial canal, are gardens and houses and in the distance is a fort from which emerge a line of troops. Beyond the main river, on top, are ranges of mountains.

43.

A prince, hunting,
meets a lady
Mughal Style,
late eighteenth century
$7\frac{1}{8} \times 11\frac{1}{4}$ inches

The prince, on horseback, with a hawk perched on the left arm, emerges from a clump of trees to see a lady, *en deshabillé*, seated on the edge of a pool with her feet resting in the water. She is accompanied by a duenna and two attendants. A row of trees in the background.

44.

Horsemen near a mountain
Mughal Style,
late eighteenth century
$7\frac{5}{8} \times 8\frac{1}{2}$ inches

Six horsemen approach a tall mountain from the left, two others from the right. The heads of all the figures are in two-thirds profile.

45.

Portrait of the third Īmām,
Hazrat Hussain
Mughal Style,
late eighteenth century
11 × 6¼ inches

The Īmām, with nimbus, rests his hands on a crutch. He wears a massive tunic and a bright red coat.

46.

An equestrian portrait
Mughal Style,
late eighteenth century
8⅝ × 6 inches

A nobleman is shown on a prancing horse. Chartreuse background; grass and floral plants in the foreground.

47.

Rāginī Naṭa
Mughal Style,
late eighteenth century
5¼ × 3⅜ inches

A soldier on horseback duels with another soldier on foot. In the foreground is a dead body. Hilly landscape with trees with circular foliage. In the center is a lake with ducks and cranes.

48–50.

Four folios from a Ms. of
the *Ālamgīr-nāma*
Mughal Style,
late eighteenth century
8⅝ × 5¾ inches

(48.) Aurangzeb receiving homage from a nobleman.
The emperor is seated on a throne beneath the canopy of a tent. Behind him are attendants carrying the *qūr* (regalia) and gifts on trays. Facing him are a group of courtiers. Beyond the enclosure, in the foreground, are horses with a groom, a doorkeeper, and a man carrying a covered tray.

(49.) Aurangzeb at the siege of a city.
In the foreground is the emperor seated on a palanquin facing a bearded horseman who is shown in a gesture of respect and supplication. Above is depicted the bombardment of the besieged town by cannon, the charge of the cavalry, and soldiers attempting to gain admission to the fort by escalade.

(50.) The double-page painting shows the court of Aurangzeb.
To the right we see him seated on the peacock throne surrounded by courtiers. To the left are more courtiers, musicians, entertainers, and riders on elephants carrying the imperial insignia.

In spite of the late date, it is interesting to note the clear survival of conventions established for these types of illustrations in the historical manuscripts of the early seventeenth century.

This manuscript is presumably a copy of the Ālamgīr-nāma and belongs to the period of Shāh Ālam (1759–1806), from which time we get several other copies of this type, notably the Shāh Jahān-nāma in the Khuda Baksh Oriental Public Library, Patna.

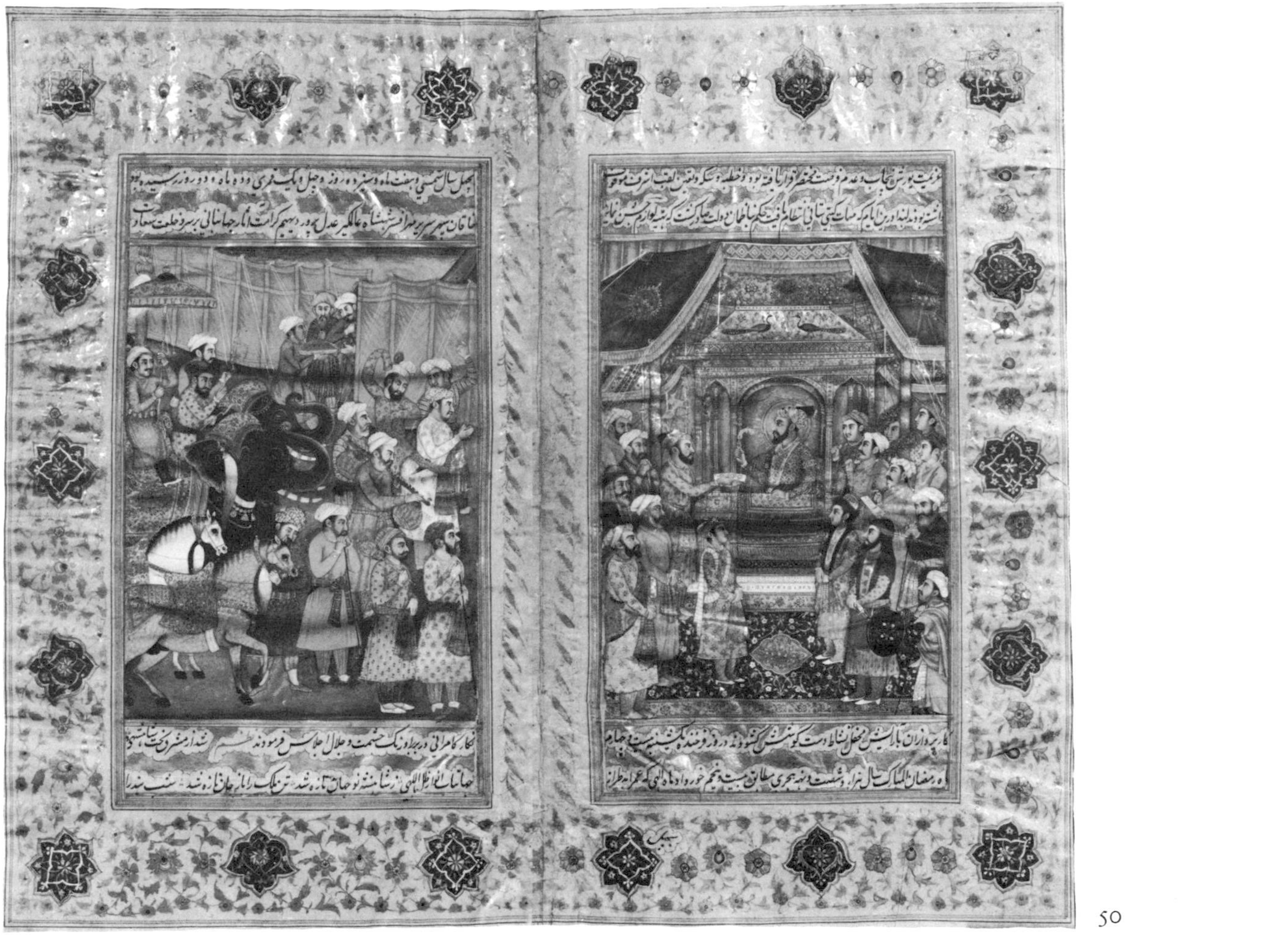

50

51.

Lovers carousing
on a terrace
Mughal Style,
late eighteenth century
$7\frac{1}{8} \times 4\frac{3}{4}$ inches

The man embraces his lady and offers her wine from a cup, while she leans back to point at the cloudy sky and the peacocks. Note the wall painting on a panel of the lower story depicting a lion and a cow. Paintings of this type are crude adaptations of earlier pictures with similar themes, some of which are as early as the reign of Jahāngīr. Cf. T.W. Arnold and J.V.S. Wilkinson, *The Chester Beatty Collection of Indian Miniatures*, Vol. III, Oxford, 1936, Pl. 56.

52.

A pair of birds
Mughal Style,
eighteenth century
$6\frac{1}{8} \times 7\frac{7}{8}$ inches

Tracings of this type, done on deer membrane, are known as *charbās* and formed part of the aids assembled by artists for future use.

53.

A black buck
Mughal Style,
late eighteenth century
$7\frac{1}{2} \times 5\frac{1}{4}$ inches

The miniature is an example of the large number of fair-to-poor copies of the original animal portraits painted during the reign of Jahāngīr. (Cf. Black buck and keeper by Manohar, Victoria and Albert Museum, No. IM 134–1921). The black buck was in strong demand, and several versions are known.

54.

Boatmen approaching a man
seated on a pedestal in the
center of a lake
Mughal Style (probably Kashmir),
early nineteenth century
$6\frac{5}{8} \times 3\frac{1}{2}$ inches

The lake is indicated by lotus flowers and leaves and large fishes. The color is bright, with orange and blue used for the dress of the figures.

55.

A hunting scene
Mughal Style,
probably late nineteenth century
$5\frac{1}{8} \times 9$ inches

A woman on horseback is shooting an arrow at fleeing deer. A man, a hawk on his forearm, is shown on horseback behind the woman. Rocks in the background.

The painting is an adaptation of an older theme. Paintings of this type were made in large numbers in the late nineteenth and early twentieth centuries at Delhi to be sold to visitors in search of curiosities.

56.

Two folios from an unidentified Ms.
Mughal Style; text, late eighteenth
century; paintings, twentieth century
$8\frac{1}{2} \times 4\frac{1}{4}$ inches

In the preparation of Mughal books, the calligrapher first wrote the text, leaving blank areas to be subsequently filled by painters who sometimes did not complete the job. Thus, one often comes across manuscripts with blank spaces. In this instance, the text is of the late eighteenth century, but the paintings have been done by a modern artist.

57.

Princess with a child,
listening to music
Twentieth-century copy of
a Mughal painting of the
eighteenth century
$6\frac{7}{8} \times 4\frac{3}{8}$ inches

The painting is a modern forgery.

58.

Aurangzeb on a boat
Twentieth-century copy of
a Mughal painting of the
late seventeenth century
$10\frac{1}{2} \times 14\frac{3}{8}$ inches

The picture is a modern copy of Cat. no. 30. No elaborate attempt has been made to deceive; the color is unabashedly modern, and the distant palm trees are distinctly reminiscent of present-day "calendar art" landscapes.

59.

A Mughal emperor
reviewing animals
Mughal Style, twentieth century
$7\frac{1}{4} \times 5\frac{1}{2}$ inches

Paintings of this type are modern versions of imagined events of the past. It is difficult to class them as forgeries, for no attempt is made to deceive anybody with the slightest knowledge.

Deccanī Style

Surviving examples of miniature painting in the Deccan date from approximately the second half of the sixteenth century. Influences from the court of Akbar, together with local elements carried over from the art of the Hindu Vijayanagara dynasty, led to the development of a distinct style at the sultanates of Ahmednagar, Bidar, Golkunda, and Bijapur. The various schools have not yet been clearly differentiated, but Bijapur, under the cultured Ibrāhīm 'Ādil Shāh II, played an important role. With the extended campaigns of Aurangzeb in the Deccan during the late seventeenth century and the subsequent establishment of the powerful kingdom of Hyderabad in 1724, Bijapur, close to Golkunda, became the most important cultural center of the Deccan. A vigorous school of painting flourished there for over a hundred years. Other local centers also grew up in the Deccan, notably at Aurangabad, Kurnool, and Shorapur. The art style patronized by the rising Maratha power, often in conflict with Hyderabad, was an adaptation of the Deccanī style. Rājasthānī influences also played a strong part in the evolution of the style. The contact with the Mughal school was always maintained.

60.

An entertainment in a garden
Deccanī Style,
early seventeenth century
$5\frac{1}{2} \times 3$ inches

The painting is considerably damaged and the color has flaked away from large areas. It was originally part of a double-page composition, the left half, preserved here, depicting two noblemen sitting beneath *chinar* trees near a stream. The foreground is filled with numerous retainers, both seated and standing, carrying trays.

61.

A lady pouring wine
Deccanī Style,
early seventeenth century
$6\frac{5}{8} \times 3\frac{1}{2}$ inches

A lady, dressed in European fashion, wearing a ruffled collar and a hat decorated with a feather, pours wine into a cup. Dark indigo background interspersed towards the bottom with delicate flowering plants, the leaves of which are touched with yellow.

62.

A *yoginī*
Deccanī Style,
early seventeenth century
$5\frac{1}{4} \times 2\frac{3}{4}$ inches

The lady clasps her hands above the head. She wears a long *jāmā* with pointed ends reaching to the ankles, a narrow *paṭkā*, and a green shawl swirling over her shoulders and flaring out at the ends. Her hair is dressed in a plain topknot and, in addition to the crossed necklace and numerous strands of pearls, she has on a garland of white flowers. The background is unpainted.

63.

Lady with a peacock
Deccanī Style,
late seventeenth century
$5\frac{3}{4} \times 3\frac{5}{8}$ inches

The bird is painted stiffly, as though it were a toy. The head is repainted.

61

62

64.

A lady receiving an attendant
Deccanī Style, mid-eighteenth century
$5\frac{5}{8} \times 3\frac{1}{4}$ inches

The lady, seated on a stool beneath a weeping willow in an open landscape, converses with a male attendant.

65.

Rāginī Varāṭī
Deccanī Style,
early eighteenth century
$9\frac{1}{8} \times 5\frac{3}{8}$ inches

A lady, her hands clasped langorously behind the head, sits on the porch of an elaborate two-story building and listens to the song of an attendant. She is approached by a maid carrying a bowl. The garden is divided into rectangular panels filled with flowers. Cloudy sky.

66.

The Emperor Aurangzeb
and a nobleman
Deccanī Style,
early eighteenth century
$5\frac{7}{8} \times 4$ inches

The aged emperor, one hand resting on a sword, is faced by a nobleman holding a rose and a chain of beads.

67.

Ladies relaxing on a terrace
Deccanī Style (Hyderabad),
early eighteenth century
$9\frac{1}{4} \times 5\frac{3}{4}$ inches

Two ladies are conversing, one of them combing her hair, the other sipping from a cup. They stand on a carpeted terrace at the edge of a pool filled with fish. In the background are elaborately ornamented buildings, and trees and flowers beyond the parapet. The drawing is elaborate and studied, almost to the point of hardness.

68.

Lady picking pomegranates
Deccanī Style,
mid-eighteenth century
$8 \times 4\frac{1}{2}$ inches

The lady, holding a flower vase in one hand and a pomegranate in the other, stands in a hilly landscape by the edge of a stream. She is accompanied by a dog. Birds hover around the bush which is loaded with fruit. A bank of craggy rocks on the horizon.

69.

Lady conversing with a duenna
Deccanī Style,
late eighteenth century
$6\frac{7}{8} \times 4\frac{7}{8}$ inches

A lady, leaning elegantly against the trunk of a tree with pale-green leaves, converses with an aged duenna who supports herself with a crutch. Pale yellow background, with a narrow strip of blue clouds and sky on the top. Flowering plants in the foreground.

Several versions of this painting are known to exist, some of them painted in the Deccan and some in Rajasthan.

70.

Kṛishṇa playing the flute
Deccanī Style (probably Shorapur),
late eighteenth century
$9\frac{7}{8} \times 7\frac{1}{8}$ inches

Kṛishṇa, seated beneath a flowering tree around which hover several birds, plays upon a flute. Several cows have gathered near and strain their necks to hear the music. A cowmaid, a pot balanced on her head, stands to the left; a cowherd, with hands folded in adoration, stands to the right. A pool of water with jagged banks is in the foreground.

71.

Lady in an open landscape
Deccanī Style,
late eighteenth century
7×5 inches

The lady, with nimbus, is seated on the forked trunk of a tree. To the left is the grave of a saint which she has apparently come to visit. Clouds in the sky, a stream in the foreground.

70

72.

Śiva and Pārvatī on
Mount Kailāsa
Deccanī Style,
early nineteenth century
$9\frac{5}{8} \times 6\frac{3}{4}$ inches

Śiva, carrying a black antelope and a trident in the upper two hands, sits on his mountain abode with Pārvatī, his consort, on his lap. The couple is attended by their son, the elephant-headed God Gaṇeśa, who waves a fly whisk. The bull Nandi crouches just below the divine couple. The mountain has caves which shelter ascetics and animals. Simple landscape with animals in the background.

Company Style

With the increasing political domination of India by the British during the nineteenth century and the changing tastes and demands of the new ruling classes, the surviving artists of the Mughal tradition in Delhi and the provinces began to adjust their work correspondingly. A style heavily influenced by the West came into being and flourished, not only at Murshidabad, Patna, and Lucknow where British influence was strong, but also in Rajasthan and the hill states of the Himalayas. This new style, called the "Company Style" because of its association with the rising power of the East India Company, spread rapidly to other parts of India under British control, including the South. Artistically its achievements are for the most part of poor quality, though fine studies of natural life were occasionally painted.

73.

The maker of bangles
Company Style (Murshidabad),
early nineteenth century
$8\frac{7}{8} \times 6\frac{1}{8}$ inches

A lady, who has taken her seat opposite the craftsman, is trying on bangles. The various tools of the trade are laid out before the man, including a fire used to shape the lacquer. In the foreground is an aged duenna, the lady's escort, and a woman nursing a child, apparently the bangle maker's wife. In the background is a tiled cottage and a creeper wound on a bamboo scaffolding.

The miniature is still close to the traditional style, but the rather cool colors represent an adjustment to the British taste.

74.

A nobleman listening to music
Company Style, c. 1870
$11\frac{5}{8} \times 16\frac{3}{4}$ inches

The man, seated on a chair, listens to a group of musicians squatting on a striped blue carpet. He is attended by several retainers, one of them about to step out of a door. The walls of the room are plain and painted a bluish white. The clothes of the musicians and the turbans of the nobleman and his retainers provide accents of color.

The carefully worked out perspective and the attempts made at modelling the clothes and the facial features show a keen desire to imitate western painting.

On the reverse is a Persian inscription.

74

75.

A painter at work
Company Style,
mid-nineteenth century
$6 \times 4\frac{1}{8}$ inches

A painter, wearing a pince-nez and surrounded by vials of paint, brushes, and other tools, is busy at work on a painting which he has placed on a stool.

Series of paintings called *firkās*, illustrating the various professions, trades and crafts, were in great demand by British residents.

76.

Portrait of a courtesan
Company Style,
late nineteenth century
$3\frac{5}{8} \times 2\frac{1}{4}$ inches

The lady stands in a heavily curtained room, one hand resting on a table, the other on the waist. The posture and setting were very popular and are invariably found in photographic portraits of this period.

77.

A bird and a flower
Company Style,
late nineteenth century
$5\frac{3}{4} \times 3\frac{7}{8}$ inches

Artists working in the Company style were often at their best in natural studies of plants and beasts. This rather roughly painted sketch still retains the decorative emphasis of Mughal work.

78.

Bullock cart at rest
Company Style,
mid-nineteenth century
Painting on mica
$3\frac{3}{4} \times 5\frac{3}{4}$ inches

The bullocks have been unyoked from the cart which carries camping equipment, including a chair. The animals are feeding and at rest, while the drivers are enjoying a smoke. A soldier, in British uniform and carrying a bayonet, is at the right.

79.

Portrait of a lady
Company Style,
mid-nineteenth century
$7 \times 4\frac{1}{8}$ inches

The lady wears a pink skirt and a white robe. She is sensitively drawn, the linear rhythms, clearly derived from the Pahāṛī style, being readily apparent in spite of the overlay of fussier technique.

79

80.

A wayside inn in
the mountains
Company Style,
mid-nineteenth century
$8 \times 5\frac{3}{8}$ inches

A woman sits outside of her hut in the shade of a tree. She holds a spouted jar with one hand and a straw fan in the other. Facing her is a traveller carrying a sword and a bundle over the shoulder. Adjoining the platform is a pool fed by a spring, and in the foreground a woman carrying pots of water. A smoking fire and a tree are in the foreground; in the background are hills and a stream.

Many elements of this painting substantially preserve features of the Kangra style, but the figures, particularly the faces, are yielding to the new taste.

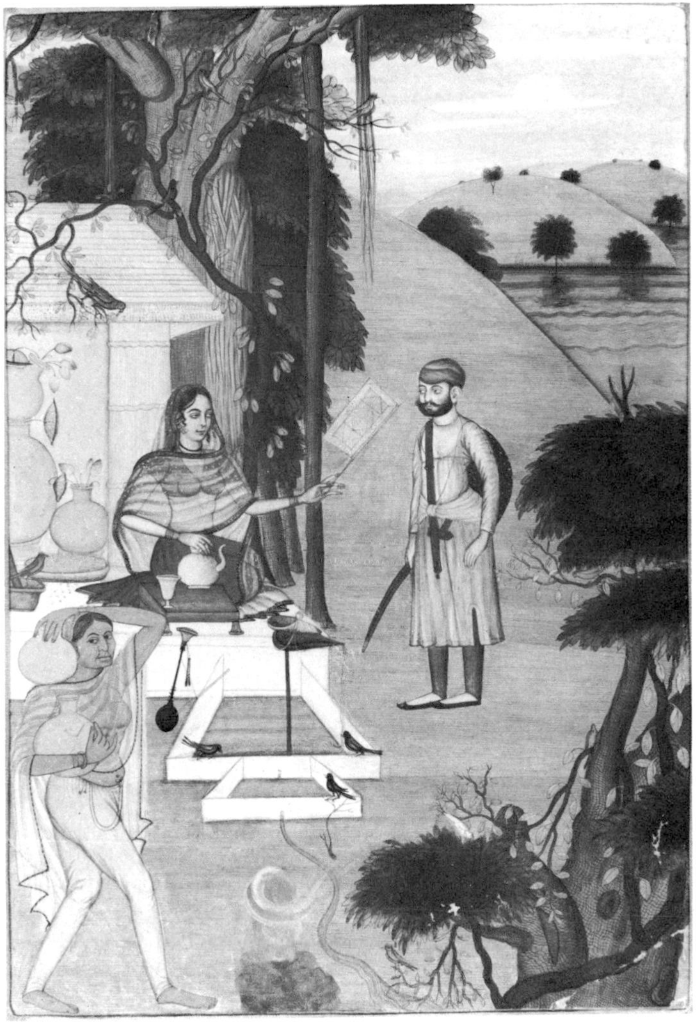

80

81.

Portrait of a Rājpūt chief
Company Style,
late nineteenth century
$6\frac{1}{2} \times 5\frac{3}{8}$ inches

The drawing of a man with sparse, parted beard and waxed moustache shows the strong influence of photography, particularly in the rendering of the face.

A very faint inscription on the top says *gafurā rāj śrī sāvant sangh jī* (Sāvant Singh of Gafurā state).

82.

Portrait of a youth
Company Style,
late nineteenth century
$5\frac{3}{8} \times 3\frac{1}{2}$ inches

As in many portraits of this type, the greatest attention is paid to the head, the rest of the body being summarily painted. The eyes are intense, the red and green turban being the only accent of color. The painting is probably the work of an artist working in South India.

Rājasthānī Style: Gujarat

As is to be expected, Gujarat, which was one of the strongest centers of the Western Indian style, retained features of that style for a period considerably longer than other areas. An early seventeenth century manuscript of the *Uttarādhyayana Sūtra* from Anjar is hardly to be distinguished from the Western Indian style, except that in some instances the "farther eye" is dropped in painting the face. Among the earliest paintings which belong to the Rājasthānī style are those illustrating a *Laghu Saṁgrahaṇī* dated A.D. 1583, to be followed by paintings of the type represented in the Catalogue (no. 83). The Gujarat school continued to flourish throughout the seventeenth and eighteenth centuries, illustrations of books continuing to be the favorite medium of expression.

REFERENCE:

MOTI CHANDRA and U.P. SHAH, "New Documents of Jaina Painting," *Śrī Mahāvīra Jaina Vidyālaya: Golden Jubilee Volume* (Bombay, 1968), pp. 348–420.

83.

The Goddess Pṛithvī lauds Kṛishṇa:
folio from a Ms. of the
Bhāgavata Purāṇa
Gujarat, early seventeenth century
$7\frac{3}{8} \times 12\frac{1}{2}$ inches

The son of Narakāsura, whose father has been slain by Kṛishṇa, prostrates himself before Kṛishṇa. Pale green background.

In style the painting resembles the *Bhāgavata Daśamskandha*, dated 1610, now in the Jodhpur Museum (K. Khandalavala, "Leaves from Rajasthan," *Mārg*, IV, No. 3 (1950), Fig. 8), and can also be dated to the early seventeenth century.

84.

Doctrine of the six *leśyas*:
folio from a Ms. of the
Saṅgrahaṇī Sūtra
Gujarat, c. 1625
$7\frac{1}{4} \times 3\frac{3}{4}$ inches

Six men, the color of their bodies ranging from black to white according to their state of spiritual progress, are seen amidst the branches of a tree. The black person, who is of the lowest spiritual stature, foolishly chops away at the trunk

of the Tree of Life; the white man, who is at the highest point of spiritual achievement, enjoys the fruits and flowers without damaging the Tree in the least. The others are shown amongst the branches, treating the Tree according to their spiritual evolution. (For a similar painting see *Khajanchi Catalogue*, Fig. 18, no. 9.)

85.

Kṛishṇa and companions playing: folio from a series illustrating the *Bhāgavata Purāṇa*
Gujarat, mid-seventeenth century
$8\frac{1}{2} \times 7$ inches

At the top are Kṛishṇa and Rādhā in a swing which is rocked by the *sakhīs*. At the bottom, we see a team composed of Rādhā and her female companions playing a game that looks like field hockey against an all-male team which consists of Kṛishṇa and the cowherds. Blue ground decorated with floral plants.

The series consisted of a large number of paintings by several hands, and is now dispersed. Cf. S.C. Welch and M. Beach, *Gods, Thrones and Peacocks*, New York, 1965, no. 15.

85

86.

Folio from a series
illustrating the *Rāmāyaṇa*
Gujarat, late eighteenth century
10 × 6 inches

On the obverse, two *chaurī* bearers attend a person holding a flower. On the reverse, Hanumān attends Sītā enthroned.

The picture, painted simply on plain paper, is in a folk idiom reminiscent of figured cloths from Gujarat.

Rājasthānī Style: Mewar

The Mewar school was among the most important in Rajasthan, the earliest dated paintings of the school being the *Rāgamālā* series painted at Chawand in 1605. About the beginning of the second quarter of the seventeenth century, the work shows an acquaintance with the Mughal painting of the reign of Jahāngīr, probably through popular Mughal intermediaries (as demonstrated by the *Rāgamālā* series of 1928 painted by Sāhabdī). The illustrations to the *Gīta Govinda* in the present collection (Cat. no. 87) belong to the school of Sāhabdī also. His atelier seems to have flourished until at least the middle of the seventeenth century. The original richness, strength and intensity of the school seems to have faded in the second half of the seventeenth century. A wave of Mughal influence began to change the style in a real sense around the opening years of the eighteenth century. Portraits, scenes of the chase and hunt, and illustrations of the sentiments of romantic poetry were the favored themes. The coloring is always bright and vivid. Though the emotional fervor of the seventeenth century was never regained, the special qualities of eighteenth century Mewāṛī painting have not yet received the recognition they deserve. The early nineteenth century continued to produce works in the tradition of the eighteenth, but the school entered a phase of decline around the middle of the nineteenth century, although one comes across good works at even this late date. Of particular importance during this period was the religious center of Nathdwara, where vast numbers of paintings were made for the pilgrim trade, and where painting in a debased traditional style continues up to the present day.

87.

Rādhā conversing with a confidante
Mewar, c. 1625
$8\frac{1}{4} \times 6\frac{3}{4}$ inches

Rādhā describes to her friend what she conceives to be the emotional state of Kṛishṇa, who is unaffected by her absence, impervious to the breezes of the Malaya mountains and the full moon, which should disturb acutely the mental states of parted lovers. The mountain and the full moon are painted in the background; in the foreground is Kṛishṇa with a group of four maidens in a wooded landscape which is indicated by a row of trees, including one with circular foliage in brilliant green and yellow, and a supple date palm on which perch a pair of birds.

The painting is very similar to the *Rāgamālā* series painted in 1628 at Udaipur during the reign of Rāṇā Jagat Singh by Sāhabdī. This painter also worked on the *Bhāgavata Purāṇa* of 1648 and the *Rāmāyaṇa* of 1648 1650.

Cf. *Khanjanchi Catalogue*, no. 23, particularly 23e, *Rāginī Sāraṅga*.

88.

Kṛishṇa surprises the *gopīs* at a game of *chaupaṛ*: illustration to a series illustrating the *Rasikapriyā* of Keśavadāsa
Mewar, mid-seventeenth century
$7\frac{1}{2} \times 7$ inches

The *gopīs*, absorbed in the game, are startled by the sudden arrival of Kṛishṇa. Bright red and orange background. The white domes of the buildings are painted against a black ground and a light blue sky. The heroine described in this situation is called *anūḍhāprakāśa nāyikā*. For a correct text of the verse inscribed on the top, see *Keśava Granthāvalī*, Allahabad, 1954, p. 18.

87

89.

The Goddess Sarasvatī
Mewar, c. 1650–1675
$3\frac{7}{8} \times 8\frac{5}{8}$ inches

The painting, probably the frontispiece of a manuscript, depicts Sarasvatī, the Goddess of Learning, seated on a lotus and holding in her four arms an elephant goad (*aṅkuśa*), a lute (*vīṇā*), a string of beads, and a book. On either side are plantain trees with flowering creepers and flowering shrubs. Red background.

90.

A folio, probably from
a series illustrating
the *Bhāgavata Purāṇa*
Mewar, c. 1675–1700
$7\frac{1}{2} \times 14\frac{3}{8}$ inches

Crowned male figures are shown with winged *apsarases* in a grove and in pavilions perched atop rocky eminences. In the foreground are princes conversing, a man extinguishing a fire, and a couple seated on a platform pointing towards a seated cow.

The miniature is similar to *Rajput Miniatures from the Collection of Edwin Binney, 3rd*, Portland, 1965, p. 24, no. 9. The style represents an unimaginative simplification of the traditions of the *Bhāgavata Purāṇa* of 1648, but is close to it in the bright coloring.

91.

Kṛishṇa embracing Rādhā
by the riverside
Mewar, early eighteenth century
$3\frac{3}{8} \times 2\frac{3}{4}$ inches

The small, brilliantly colored miniature shows Kṛishṇa, with nimbus, wearing a golden skirt over the bright yellow *pītāmbar*. He holds Rādhā's hand, one arm resting on her shoulder. The dark Yamunā flows behind, and in it is an empty golden pavilion surrounded by pink and white lotuses. The river is dammed by a bund. Fish leap over the falling water. At its side is a cluster of three trees with dark foliage touched with pink and yellow, and clasped by white-flowered creepers; across it stumble a group of cows, slipping in the water as they go. In the background, on the farther shore, is a horizontal row of trees with dense foliage relieved with bright spots of color, and in the center a bright green and yellow plantain tree with a deep crimson flower. Above the trees are clouds tinted pink, blue, and gold, and a narrow strip of sky.

The painting is similar in style to a *Bhāgavata Purāṇa* series illustrated by Moti Chandra, *Mewar Painting*, Pl. 10, but of more delicate and finer workmanship. It is the Rājasthānī counterpart of the gorgeous Mughal style of the early seventeenth century as seen in the *Gīta Govinda* folio of the Cowasji Jehangir Collection (K. Khandalavala and Moti Chandra, *Collection of Sir Cowasji Jehangir*, no. 16, p. 17).

92.

Folio from a Ms.
of the *Nemipurāṇa*
Probably Mewar,
early eighteenth century
$4\frac{5}{8} \times 4\frac{1}{8}$ inches

The Tīrthaṅkara, seated cross-legged on a throne provided with a parasol, is adored by a naked monk and other worshippers. A label above the painting reads: *nemanāthjī nailavanta rūpu chhai* (Neminatha is blue in color).

91

93.

Mahārāṇā Jagat Singh II (1734–1751) of Mewar at the festival of Holi
Mewar, c. 1740
$16\frac{1}{4} \times 10\frac{1}{2}$ inches

It is a Rājasthānī custom for the retainers of the ruling chief to call upon him during the festival of Holi, and ceremonially hold a mirror before him. It is thus we see the Rāṇā seated on the terrace of a palace by a hillside. In the first enclosure is an elephant in a stable, and outside the walls are soldiers carrying regal paraphernalia, entertainers, elephants and horses—all part of the procession in which the Rāṇā rode out to the palace for the ceremony.

93

94.

Mahārāṇā Jagat Singh II
(1734–1751) of Mewar in procession
Mewar, c. 1740
$8\frac{5}{8} \times 8\frac{7}{8}$ inches

The Rāṇā, with nimbus, is shown on the back of an elephant which he drives himself. Flanking him are two elephants, each of which is mounted by a *chaurī* bearer; while behind is yet another elephant with a courtier who turns to face him, hands folded in a gesture of respect.

In the foreground are retainers on foot carrying the regalia and a groom with two hounds on leash. Dark green background.

Mahārāṇā Jagat Singh was well known for his love of elephants. J. Tod, *Annals and Antiquities of Rajasthan*, Oxford, 1920, vol. I, p. 492 reproduces the translation of a letter from the Rāṇā to his chief agent in the midst of negotiations with the Marathas on the outcome of which depended peace or war. The king expresses grave concern for the political situation, but does not fail to mention the noble fight between his elephants and also the "thousand pranks of Sundar Gaj."

94

95.

Laylā visits Majnūn
Mewar, mid-eighteenth century
$8\frac{1}{4} \times 5\frac{1}{2}$ inches

The painting is obviously after a Mughal miniature of the Akbar or Jahāngīr period. It shows the emaciated lover conversing with his beloved who is accompanied by two female attendants carrying fly whisks of peacock feathers (*morchhals*). To the left is a seated camel with a litter on top, accompanied by a resting groom. Further down is an unyoked bullock cart, slumbering drivers, soldiers, and an emaciated horse. In the lower right corner are mountains amidst which is a village and two farmers. In the background is a range of hills with mountain rams and a figure carrying a circular object, obviously imitating the curious forms, both animal and figural, which the shapes of mountains and rocks take on in Mughal painting. The fort perched on the mountain is obviously Chittor with the Kīrttistambha (Tower of Victory) clearly visible.

Some of the Mughal influence to be seen in eighteenth-century Rājasthānī painting is due to Mughal work of an earlier period which was present in local collections and available to Rājasthānī painters.

95

96.

Folio from a series illustrating
the *Satsaī* of Bihārī
Mewar, mid-eighteenth century
$7\frac{3}{8} \times 7\frac{1}{8}$ inches

In the upper story of the pavilion to the right is Kṛishṇa conversing with a lady. In the lower story are two women, also in conversation. Rādhā is shown walking by the banks of a river with conventional lotus flowers and foliage and geese.

Superscribed is a verse from the *Satsaī*, numbered 425. The painting belongs to a large series which should have consisted of 700 paintings when complete. These are now scattered among numerous collections throughout the world.

97.

A lady shoots a tiger while
embraced by her beloved
Mewar, mid-eighteenth century
$7\frac{1}{2} \times 5\frac{1}{2}$ inches

The lady turns around to shoot the striped animal. The man wears a turban of the Maratha type, indicating the growing impact of the Marathas in Rajasthan at this time.

98.

The elephant Nakhatulā
Mewar, mid-eighteenth century
$7\frac{7}{8} \times 6\frac{1}{8}$ inches

The elephant is ridden by a mahout carrying two goads, one in each hand. Blue background with clumps of green grass in the foreground.

The inscription on the red top margin reads: *Hāthī Nakhatulā* (the elephant Nakhatulā). Another inscription on the reverse reads: *mhārāṇā śrī rāj sīghji kī vaṝakau* (Mahārāṇā Rāj Singh II ruled Mewar from A.D. 1754–1761).

99.

A pair of dogs, and
a hawk on a perch
Mewar, late eighteenth century
$9\frac{3}{4} \times 4\frac{3}{4}$ inches

Large floral plants are interspersed on the background.

100.

Two studies of a seated boy
Mewar, late eighteenth century
$4\frac{7}{8} \times 3$ inches

The boy is probably an apprentice learning to paint.

101.

An artist at work
Mewar, c. 1800
$7\frac{1}{8} \times 6\frac{1}{8}$ inches

The painter is seated, the right leg tucked under the thigh, the left stretched out. He rests the board with the paper on his right thigh and is working with a brush. A pot, a box, a vial, and brush cases are placed around him.

102.

Mahārāṇā Bhīm Singh (1778–1828)
of Mewar on a hunt
Mewar, early nineteenth century
$5\frac{3}{4} \times 5\frac{1}{8}$ inches

The Mahārāṇā, dressed in green, stands with a hawk perched on his gloved left hand. Facing him are retainers with hands folded in respect. In the foreground is a servant skinning a slain duck.

103.

The festival of Holi in
the Śrīnāthadvārā temple
Mewar (Nathdwara), c. 1830
$8\frac{3}{8} \times 6$ inches

On top, the chief priest scatters colored powder on the image which is specially decorated for the occasion. A pair of syringes, used for squirting colored water, lie at the feet of the image. Below we see the priest again, attending the image of the child Kṛishṇa whose throne is surrounded by plantains with bluish leaves and other foliage. Male and female worshippers hold a tray of colored water and a pouch filled with colored powder. Musicians playing on cymbals, *pakhāvaj* and *ḍaph*, are presumably singing songs of the Holi festival.

104.

The temple at Śrīnāthadvārā
Mewar (Nathdwara),
mid-nineteenth century
$5\frac{7}{8} \times 3\frac{7}{8}$ inches

The temple is enclosed by a wall, and contains images of the Deity in various forms, as well as groups of worshippers. In the compound are smaller buildings with images of other divinities. Outside the first enclosure are devotees engaged in the performance of ritual.

105.

A hunting scene
Mewar, mid-nineteenth century
$7\frac{1}{8} \times 13\frac{3}{4}$ inches

A hawk has pounced upon a black buck along a stream that issues from a swampy lake. Two hunters, camouflaged with a dress of leaves, run in the direction of the animal. Cranes are perched on the edges of the lake from which startled birds take to flight.

The inscription on the reverse reads:
4 *śrī sāhaujādo ki sakāḍ*
chatārā paimjī kī kalam
(No. 4 The prince on a hunt. Work of the painter Paimjī [Premjī]).

106.

Mahārāṇā Śambhū Singh
(1861–1874) in procession
Mewar, c. 1875
$10\frac{1}{2} \times 14\frac{1}{2}$ inches

The young Rāṇā, seated on an elephant with gorgeous trappings, is attended by a nobleman waving a *chaurī*. His retinue consists of soldiers and retainers carrying the full regalia.

The inscription on the top margin reads:
mahārājādhirāj mahārāṇā śrī sambhūs-yangh jī
savārī mā hāthī bādalāsaṇagār pāche
rāvat khumāṇ sanghjī
(Mahārājādhirāj Mahārāṇā Śambhū Singh on the elephant Bādlāsaṇagār [Bādalśringār]. Behind him is Rāvat Khumān Singh.)

107.

Hunting tigers in
mountainous terrain
Mewar, late nineteenth century
$11\frac{1}{8} \times 15\frac{7}{8}$ inches

The hills are painted with simple rows of trees. A nobleman shoots a tiger from a watch tower by a dam.

106

108.

Studies of European figures
Mewar, mid-nineteenth century
$4\frac{1}{2} \times 4\frac{1}{8}$ inches

The study sheet shows four European figures, one of them seated on a chair and three busts. The artist seems to have been trying to acquaint himself with unfamiliar anatomies, and also with the shapes of European caps.

109.

Śrī Nāthajī in Goloka
Mewar (Nathdwara),
mid-nineteenth century
Painting on cloth
$52 \times 40\frac{1}{2}$ inches

Within an enclosure, along the walls of which are rows of cows, stands Kṛishṇa as Śrī Nāthajī adored by cowmaids and showered with flowers by Gods seated in aerial chariots. Beyond the lower wall is a stream with lotuses and fishes.

Large paintings on cloth of this type were generally hung behind the image in temples of the Vallabha cult.

109

Rājasthānī Style: Bundi and Kotah

A school certainly as important as Mewar, and perhaps more so, developed in Bundi and in the neighboring state of Kotah, which was ruled by a younger branch of the Bundi family. The earliest examples of the style are represented by a *Rāgamālā* series, now dispersed, probably dating from the end of the sixteenth century. From its very inception, the Bundi style seems to have derived a greater inspiration from the Mughal school, particularly in its strong feeling for movement. This quality distinguishes all work done in these states from painting in other parts of Rajasthan right up to the nineteenth century. The history of Bundi painting in the first half of the seventeenth century is unclear, but the second half was a period of considerable productivity. The end of the seventeenth century and the beginning of the next provided works of splendid quality (Cat. no. 110). The sister state of Kotah began to produce works in a style closely allied to that of Bundi from about the same time, and the style rapidly gained in strength and authority, the splendid scenes of hunt and sport being unparalleled in Rājasthānī art. This momentum carries the school right into the nineteenth century when the quality of work, compared to that of other areas, was surprisingly fine.

REFERENCES:

W. G. ARCHER, *Indian Painting in Bundi and Kotah* (London, 1959).
PRAMOD CHANDRA, *Bundi Painting* (New Delhi, 1959).

110.

Rādhā afraid: miniature from a series illustrating the *Rasikapriyā* of Keśavadāsa
Bundi, late seventeenth century
$10\frac{1}{4} \times 6\frac{7}{8}$ inches

Rādhā, frightened by the flash of lightning all around, clings to Kṛishṇa in a pavilion, the upper story of which has a room with an empty bed. Outside is a dense grove of trees, and the sky is completely covered with tumultuous and thundering clouds strangely lit by the serpentine flashes of lightning. The seeming proximity of the lightning is suggested by showing an individual bolt entering the room in which the lovers embrace. An exceptionally fine painting, it captures the colors and mood of a monsoon thunderstorm with urgency and immediacy.

For a slightly later *Rasikapriyā* series see A. Banerji, "Illustrations of the Rasikapriyā from Bundi-Kotah," *Lalit Kalā*, 3–4 (1957–58), pp. 67–73.

111.

Lady with attendants
on a terrace
Bundi, end of the
seventeenth century
$11\frac{3}{8} \times 7$ inches

The heroine leans against a bolster, her head turned towards the standing attendant who holds a peacock-feather fly whisk. Another attendant sits with her hands folded in a respectful gesture.

Textile patterns are delineated with great delicacy. The architecture is rich and sumptuous, and the trees in the background, including the mango in fruit, the slender palms and creepers, and a dark leaved tree inhabited by birds are painted against a rich blue sky.

For a correct version of the superscribed text, see *Keśava Granthāvalī*, vol. 1, p. 6, verses 9 and 10.

111

112.

Śiva and Pārvatī
Bundi, end of the
seventeenth century
$4\frac{3}{8} \times 4\frac{1}{4}$ inches

The God, wearing a skull necklace, converses patiently with his consort. They are both seated on a tiger skin. Nandi, the vehicle of the God, rests on the banks of a stream.

The picture is a fragment of a larger composition.

113.

Rāginī Dhanāśrī
Bundi, end of the seventeenth
or early eighteenth century
$7\frac{5}{8} \times 4\frac{1}{2}$ inches

A lady, of green complexion, is shown painting a portrait of her beloved. In contrast to the usual Bundi manner, the architecture is relatively plain. Archaistic mannerisms survive in the posture of the lady, who is shown sitting on the upper edge of the carpet. For a painting very similar in style see *Khajanchi Catalogue*, p. 38.

114.

Rāginī Lalit
Probably Bundi,
early eighteenth century
$7\frac{7}{8} \times 4\frac{1}{2}$ inches

In the treatment of the architecture, the tiled floor pattern, and the figural types, the picture is strongly reminiscent of the Bundi school though not painted in the orthodox manner, and lacking its brilliant coloring and refined detail. It is possible that the painting may belong to Uniara where a variant of the Bundi style developed in the late eighteenth century.

115.

Rāga Vasant
Bundi or Kotah, c. 1725
$9 \times 5\frac{3}{4}$ inches

Kṛishṇa, holding a spouted jar filled with flowers and twigs in one hand and a *vīṇā* in the other, dances vigorously to the accompaniment of three female musicians. The ground is painted in a strong orange-yellow, unusual even for this style which has a preference for bright color. The large and simple flowering plants on the horizon, the bold decorative work, and

114

the simple composition suggests a child-like vision of the universe.

116.

Three folios from an illustrated
Ms. of the *Bhagavad-Gītā*
Bundi or Kotah, second quarter of the eighteenth century
$9\frac{1}{8} \times 5\frac{3}{8}$ inches

Two of the folios are illustrated. One of them shows Kṛishṇa and Rādhā in a bower by the river, the other the *rāsamaṇḍala*, with the divine lovers in the center, and Kṛishṇa alternating with the *gopīs* in the dancing group around the couple. Vigorously painted arabesques and floral patterns decorate the margins.

The writing is clear, and the text correct. The manuscript is one of the earliest illustrated examples of the *Bhagavad-Gītā*, though late examples of the nineteenth century abound.

117.

The auspicious sight of Rādhā
Probably Bundi, c. 1750–1775
$9 \times 5\frac{1}{2}$ inches

Kṛishṇa, on horseback, turns around in the saddle to peer through a dense grove of plantain trees. He sees Rādhā, who crouches shyly under cover of a shawl stretched hastily by the wary maids. The picture is painted in dull green, the accents of color being provided by the red of the skirt with bold chevron pattern, the clump of clothes on the ground, and the bright dress of Kṛishṇa.

The painting is related in color to Cat. no. 114 and is again not in the orthodox Bundi manner. It could possibly belong to the Uniara idiom.

118.

Rāga Śrī
Bundi or Kotah, c. 1780
$7 \times 4\frac{5}{8}$ inches

A musician, holding a *vīṇā*, is seated on an elaborate throne and leans against a crimson bolster. A *chaurī* bearer in chartreuse and yellow is in attendance. A graybeard dressed in white and a musician in blue are playing on a *vīṇā* and singing. In the background is a tree with dense foliage, fountains bordered by a blue tiled platform and the glowing evening sky with a pair of flying geese. The painting is gorgeously colored, the rich variety of textures suggested indicates a moment of considerable opulence in the history of the style.

The painting is similar to the one reproduced in Archer, *Indian Painting in Bundi and Kotah*, Fig. 41, which shows Rājā Durjansāl hunting and is dated A.D. 1778.

118

119.

A lady on her way
to the tryst
Bundi or Kotah,
late eighteenth century
$7\frac{1}{2} \times 5\frac{1}{8}$ inches

The lady, with skirts gently raised, walks towards the dense forest in which is shown the waiting lover. A city with a large gate is in the background. The margins are exceptionally decorative, filled with drawings of birds and plants.

119

120.

Rāginī Naṭa
Bundi, late eighteenth century
$7\frac{1}{8} \times 5$ inches

A lady, wearing a coat of mail and seated on an armored horse with elephant mask, flourishes a scimitar against a footman who wields a broad sword. In the foreground lies a bleeding, dead soldier; and in the background, to the left, is a tree with multi-colored leaves, probably a mango, and yet another tree with bluish-green leaves tinged with red. The sky is brilliant with variegated clouds, the colors having the same vivid quality as in Cat. no. 118.

120

121.

Man in a garden
Bundi, late eighteenth century
$7\frac{5}{8} \times 5\frac{1}{4}$ inches

The man, seated in a chair with a reclining back, holds a small *tānpūrā* over his shoulder. In front of him is a large *hukkā* on a stand, the smoking tube reaching for the singer's lips with a life all its own. In the foreground are plants with white flowers, and on the weeping willow are perched two birds.

One type of Bundi work of the late eighteenth century, of which this picture is an example, is noted for its soft, muted color and the generous use of grays and dull greens. Bright reds, yellows, oranges, and pinks which are characteristic of the Bundi school seem to have been consciously avoided.

122.

Procession by a palace
Bundi, late eighteenth century
$8\frac{1}{2} \times 6$ inches

The drawing depicts a group of elephants, some of them equipped with large howdahs filled with musicians. Some musicians are also shown on foot and on horseback. The attitudes of the elephant riders, many of whom turn to look behind, their hands raised in animated gestures, suggest that the group is part of a royal progress. Ladies at palace balconies and windows point with their hands at the marching group, probably showering flowers.

123.

Rām Singh II (1827–1865)
of Kotah in a procession
Kotah, mid-nineteenth century
$12\frac{1}{4} \times 19\frac{1}{8}$ inches

The king is seated on a howdah atop an elaborately caparisoned elephant. The beast supports a cage on his tusks in which dances a girl. The mahout in front of the king, and the prince seated behind, who is probably Śatrusāl his son, wave large fly whisks. At the head of the procession is a European-style band behind which are retainers carrying pennants and insignia. They are followed by a small group of Indian musicians playing on drums and *sārangīs* (fiddle) with a dancing girl in their midst. In addition to troops with fixed bayonets dressed in the fashion of European-trained soldiery, there are numerous others, some carrying swords, others guns. The rear is brought up by a covered palanquin with a lattice window, probably containing the queen.

The king is apparently passing through the clothing market, the shops displaying brightly colored saris. On the terrace are groups of women and some playful children.

The painting is very similar to the procession in the Victoria and Albert Museum, London (Archer, *Indian Painting in Bundi and Kotah*, Fig. 48), but of somewhat coarser workmanship.

123

124.

The auspicious sight of Rādhā
Kotah, mid-nineteenth century
12 × 8¼ inches

Kṛishna, with large, lotus-petal eyes, is conceived as Śrī Nāthjī, and is shown seated on a balcony holding a bud and blossom in the right hand. The long pigtail ripples behind his head, and a yellow scarf flutters in the air as he bends down to catch a glimpse of Rādhā. She is shown in the act of draping herself with a bright yellow garment as she admires her beauty in a mirror held by an attendant. On the floor, paved with mauve and blue tiles, are large silver utensils; in the background is a lush garden with plantain trees in flower. In its shelter, monkeys, birds, and squirrels scamper down tree trunks. Peacocks idle gracefully on top of the building to the right. Monkeys are at play there, and a parrot clings to a rolled-up curtain. A pair of geese fly in the sky. Amorous parrots and pigeons are to be seen on the terrace and the eaves above the doorway of the building in which Kṛishṇa is seated.

The reign of Rām Singh of Kotah (1827–1865) coincides with a period of flourishing artistic activity that extended

124

itself late into the nineteenth century when other schools of Indian miniature paintings were moribund or dead. A large number of miniatures were painted, many of them concerned with the pompous if naïve life of the ruler. The quality varied from the energetic and lively hunting scenes that retained to an astonishing degree the vigor of the Bundi style of the mid-eighteenth century to the rather static but brilliant processionals like Cat. no. 123. The lyricism of the earlier style was also retained as in this example, and the introduction of new colors, like the bright green of the halo of Kṛishṇa, was handled with unerring skill. Pictures like this display a religious intensity that is much more moving than the rather heavy and weary sensuousness of the last quarter of the eighteenth century.

125.

A throne cover
Kotah, mid-nineteenth century
$38\frac{5}{8} \times 22$ inches

On top, flanking a large bolster on which is perched a peacock, are pairs of *gopīs* with pots on their heads. Below the broad plain field in the center are six *gopīs* in a register, three in each group.

Throne covers of this type, called *simhāsanas*, are used to cover the altars on which the images of Kṛishṇa are placed in temples of the Pushṭimārga sect. Cf. Cat. no. 218.

126.

A European gentleman
Kotah, mid-nineteenth century
$3\frac{1}{2} \times 2\frac{1}{8}$ inches

The redheaded gentleman in white trousers, red coat, and black hat sits on a chair with foliate legs. He holds a cane and sniffs a flower. The bright clouds in the sky are lined with gold.

127.

A tiger hunt
Kotah, dated V.S. 1925/A.D. 1868
$14\frac{3}{4} \times 20\frac{5}{8}$ inches
The large drawing, a sketch study made on the spot, carries numerous notes indicating the names of the persons present.

Tigers are being driven from a forested ravine out into the open by numerous beaters playing trumpets, drums, and other instruments. In the bend of the river are several boats. The largest of them, provided with a canopy and chairs, is the boat of the king, empty but for the inscribed names of the persons who were present. To the left is a smaller boat, similarly empty, again carrying the names of the persons by whom it was occupied. To the far left is yet another boat carrying male and female musicians whose figures have been already sketched in.

The date of the painting indicated that the king, simply called *śrī darbār* in one of the labels, was Śatrusāl II (1865–1888), son of Rām Singh II.

128.

Śatrusāl II (1865–1888)
shooting tigers
Kotah, c. 1875
$11\frac{1}{2} \times 18\frac{3}{4}$ inches

The sketch shows the king shooting a tiger that has been ensnared by beaters, a large group of whom are to the left, one of them slashing at a boar.

129.

Elephants fighting
Kotah, early nineteenth century
$5\frac{1}{4} \times 4\frac{1}{2}$ inches

An attempt is being made to separate the battling elephants by retainers who are setting off fireworks near the creatures. Troops and cavalry with lances can be seen in the background.

Rājasthānī Style: Malwa

Though paintings ascribed to Malwa present an unusually archaistic appearance, the earliest examples known belong to the second quarter of the seventeenth century. A *Rasikapriyā* of Keśavadāsa, now dispersed, is dated 1634, and is followed by a series of paintings illustrating the *Amarū Śataka*, dated 1652, and a *Rāgamālā*, dated 1680. All of these are done in a conservative manner, the compositions divided into registers and panels, and filled with monochrome patches of color against which are painted the rather flat and abstract figures. This distinctive style apparently came to an end towards the close of the seventeenth century or the opening years of the eighteenth, the last known example being a *Bhāgavat Purāṇa*, dated 1688. The course of its development during the eighteenth century is largely unknown, but it appears to have cast off the archaistic mannerisms and to parallel more closely developments in other parts of Rajasthan. Some scholars have suggested that the so-called "Malwa school" is erroneously assigned to Malwa on the strength of a single inscription which refers to a city that may not be in Malwa. This place is called Narsyangsahar, "the city of Narasiṁha," and there is no particular reason to identify it with Narsinghgarh in Malwa, there being several cities in India with this name.

REFERENCES:

W. G. ARCHER, *Central Indian Painting* (London and New York, 1958).

ANAND KRISHNA, *Malwa Painting* (Benares, no date).

130–131.

Two miniatures from
a *Rāgamālā* series
Malwa, third quarter of
the seventeenth century
$5\frac{3}{8} \times 5\frac{3}{8}$ inches

(130.) Rāginī Vasant
The Rāginī, personified as a blue-complexioned warrior holding a sword at the shoulder in one hand with a bird of black color perched on the other, faces a flowering grove symbolized by three trees entwined with creepers. Two large peacocks are perched on the branches. The female attendant carries a *vīṇā*. At the bottom of the picture is a register with a flowering arabesque, considered by some to be a hall-mark of the style.

Sanskrit inscription on top which gives the iconographical form of the Rāginī. It is no. 22 of a series.

(131.) Rāginī Āsāvarī
A lady, of dark brown complexion and dressed in feathers, holds a serpent that has wound itself around her hand. She is seated facing a tree, the trunk of which is clasped by more serpents. A tiger rests in its lair and monkeys are at play among the stylized trees on top. Floral arabesque at the bottom of the picture.

Sanskrit inscription on top gives the iconographical form. It is no. 33 of the same series as Cat. no. 130.

132.

Rāginī Kedāra
Malwa,
late seventeenth century
$5\frac{3}{4} \times 6$ inches

A king, who has dismounted from his horse, stands before an ascetic with hands folded in adoration. Yet another ascetic is seen at worship in the temple to the right.

The painting is related to the Kanoria *Bhāgavata Purāṇa*, dated 1686–1688 (Archer, *Indian Paintings from Rajasthan*,

131

1957, pl. VI, no. 16). The white is flaking badly, a characteristic also to be seen in the portion of the same manuscript dated 1686.

133.

Rāginī Vilāval
Malwa,
late seventeenth century
$7\frac{1}{4} \times 5$ inches

A lady, seated on a couch, completes her toilet by adjusting an earring, while a maid stands before her holding a mirror. The building has striped domes, and at the bottom of the picture are niches with bottles and cups.

The rather pale pink and gray would indicate a date immediately after the *Rāgamālā* series dated 1680 in the National Museum of India, Delhi. Cf. Khandalavala, "Leaves from Rajasthan," *Mārg*, IV (1950), Fig. 25.

133

134.

Rāginī Vilāval
Malwa, c. 1700
$8\frac{1}{2} \times 5\frac{1}{2}$ inches

Similar to Cat. no. 133. The lady's reflection in the mirror has been also painted. A conventional lotus pond in the foreground.

134

135.

Rāginī Mālaśrī
Probably Malwa,
early eighteenth century
$9\frac{1}{8} \times 6\frac{1}{8}$ inches

The lady, with nimbus, holding a *vīṇā* and a lotus, is seated on a terrace adjoining a garden. In the background are trees with peacocks, birds and a monkey.

The Malwa school finally begins to shed its archaistic mannerisms in this painting, but memories of the earlier style survive in the bright red niche on the palace wall and the treatment of trees, creepers, birds and monkeys in the background.

135

136–137.

Two miniatures from a *Rāgamālā* series
Probably Malwa, early eighteenth century
$9\frac{1}{2} \times 5\frac{3}{4}$ inches

(136.) Rāginī Guṇakalī
The lady, holding a flower, is seated on a carpet near a profusely flowering shrub. Green ground. In the foreground is a conventional lotus lake and trees and flowers. In the background a temple shaded by trees. Silver, now tarnished, is profusely used in the coloring of the trees. Bright yellow margins with arabesques in green of a type popular with artists of the Malwa school.

(137.) Rāginī Vairāṭī
The lady is shown dancing to the beat of cymbals played by an attendant.

On the reverse are two verses, one in Hindi and the other in Sanskrit. The Hindi verse is by the poet Lachhamandās.

136

Rājasthānī Style: Marwar

Little is known of Marwar painting in the early seventeenth century except for a *Rāgamālā* series painted at Pali in 1623. During the second half of the seventeenth century, the Marwar school appears to have been similar to that of Mewar, except for the colors which tend to be more somber and dark. Some paintings of the Marwar rulers, strongly dependent on the Mughal style, are also known and may well have been done under local patronage. The fine portraits and court scenes produced during the reigns of Ajit Singh (1707–1734) and his successors seem to have built on this tradition. Besides these, we have the usual scenes of hunt and sport, and the representations of themes inspired by love poetry. Paintings of the nineteenth century, though highly stylized and mannered (Cat. no. 154), are sometimes quite attractive. The extraordinary quantity produced, however, was hardly conducive to a consistently high level of achievement.

Among the *ṭhikānās* (baronies) of Marwar, Ghanerao and Nagaur apparently had flourishing idioms of their own —at least for limited periods of time. Some extremely fine portraits of the Ghanerao chiefs painted during the early eighteenth century have been discovered. Nagaur, whose masters seized the Marwar throne in the mid-eighteenth century, seems to have possessed a flourishing Jaina community that patronized the illustration of books and letters-of-invitation (*vijñaptipatras*) to religious heads.

REFERENCES:

SANGRAM SINGH, "An Early Rāgamālā Ms. from Pali (Marwar School) dated A.D. 1623," *Lalit Kalā*, 7 (April 1960), pp. 76–81.

Khajanchi Catalogue, pp. 18, 45–48.

138.

Chariot drawn by
a pair of bulls
Probably Marwar, c. 1650–1675
$5\frac{3}{4} \times 5\frac{3}{4}$ inches

The closed carriage, in the shape of a pavilion with gilt roof, is occupied by a lady painted against a chocolate ground. The charioteer, dressed in yellow, holds a whip. The undercarriage is again painted chocolate. Deep indigo ground.

The facial types, with petal-shaped eyes and pupils marked in the center, are reminiscent of the Mewar school of the mid-seventeenth century and a little later; but the dark, rich coloring is quite distinctive and probably indicates a Marwar origin.

139.

A king and courtier
conversing with holy men
Probably Marwar, c. 1650–1675
$3\frac{7}{8} \times 4\frac{1}{2}$ inches

Against a red background are shown two rows of figures. On the top is a prince, leaning against a bolster, in conversation with a Brahman, who is bare above the waist except for a necklace and the sacred thread. Below is an ascetic, with beard and *jaṭā*, holding up a book. He is in conversation with a man seated opposite, who is accompanied by two attendants. The coloring is rich, but sombre, in the tradition of Cat. no. 138.

139

140.

A lady at her toilet
Probably Marwar, c. 1650–1675
$6\frac{1}{2} \times 6\frac{1}{8}$ inches

A nude lady stands on a stool, holding up her long hair from which falls droplets of water drunk by a bird. Facing the lady is an attendant holding up a tray full of cosmetics. Deep indigo-blue ground.

A third of the picture, to the right, is missing, so that all we see is a lady painted against a brown ground, apparently in conversation with a person now entirely lost. The building originally had three domes.

The painting is related to Cat. nos. 138 and 139 in color, and all three are probably of the same provenance, though of different dates.

141.

Folio from a *Kalpasūtra* Ms.
Probably Marwar, c. 1650–1675
$4\frac{1}{2} \times 7\frac{7}{8}$ inches

To the left, in the large panel, is the mother of the Tīrthaṅkara reclining on a couch. The other smaller panels are filled with representations of the fourteen auspicious objects seen by her in the dream that announces her divine motherhood. These are, (top row) an elephant, a bull, a lion, the Goddess Śrī, a pair of garlands, the moon; (central row) the sun, a banner, a vase, and a lotus lake; (bottom row) a ship, a heavenly mansion, a heap of jewels, and a smokeless fire.

142.

Ḍholā conversing with Umar Sumrā
Marwar, early eighteenth century
$6\frac{1}{4} \times 8\frac{1}{2}$ inches

The painting is done in a folk tradition, with a thin wash of color and summary drawing.

143.

A king listening to music
Probably Marwar,
early eighteenth century
$8\frac{3}{8} \times 5\frac{1}{4}$ inches

The king, accompanied by a *chaurī* bearer, listens to a singer accompanied by a musician. They are all standing under an orange and green canopy with yellow border. Dark brown background. At the bottom are arched niches with floral patterns.

The Devanāgarī inscription on top is not legible.

144.

Lady with attendants
in a palace garden
Marwar, c. 1725–1750
10×6 inches

Two attendants, holding a bowl and a tray of flowers, stand opposite the lady. In the foreground are flower beds, bordered by a row of conventional flowering plants. The palace is elaborately painted with floral and geometric patterns.

145.

The month of Māgha:
illustration to a verse from
the *Kavipriyā* of Keśavadāsa
Marwar, mid-eighteenth century
$11\frac{1}{4} \times 6\frac{3}{4}$ inches

A nobleman, gorgeously attired, is offered a bowl of flowers by a lady who is accompanied by two others, one of them carrying a fly whisk and the other a bowl of flowers. The architecture is elaborately decorated, and the trees, inhabited by peacocks, are drawn against a bright pink wall. Beyond is Kṛishṇa, dancing to the accompaniment of a female orchestra.

The color is bright, in various shades of red, pink, yellow, and green.

The superscription, in white ink on a black ground, carries the verse of which the painting is an illustration. See *Keśava Granthāvalī*, vol. 2, p. 159.

145

146.

Equestrian portrait of a boy
Marwar, mid-eighteenth century
$8\frac{1}{4} \times 6$ inches

The boy, wearing a large, loosely wound turban and a *jāmā* reaching to the ankles, sits gravely on a horse whose head is secured by a tie-down.

147.

Portrait of
Mahārājā Rām Singh of Jodhpur
Marwar, mid-eighteenth century
$9\frac{3}{4} \times 5\frac{3}{8}$ inches

The Mahārājā, dressed in white, holds an aigrette in one hand; the other hand rests on a sword. He wears an unusually tall turban and large earrings. Gray background.

Rām Singh succeeded his father Abhai Singh (1734–1749) to the throne in 1749, but lost Jodhpur in 1751 to his uncle, the parricide Bakht Singh of Nagaur. He attempted a comeback with the help of the Marathas. As a result of the treaty of Nagaur, concluded in 1756 between the Marathas and Vijay Singh, son of Bakht Singh, Rām Singh obtained almost half of Jodhpur together with Jalor where he ruled until the year of his death, 1772.

For other portraits, see *Binney Catalogue*, Fig. 33, incorrectly assigned to 1840, and Archer, *Indian Painting*, Oxford, 1957, pl. 10.

Devanāgarī inscription on the reverse: *māhārāj śrī ramsīghjī rī sabī*, and the initials B.L.R. in English.

148.

Jaina monks addressing
the laity; fragment of
a *vijñaptipatra*
Nagaur, mid-eighteenth century
$20\frac{3}{4} \times 7\frac{7}{8}$ inches

Above is a Jaina pontiff, enthroned and fanned by an attendant holding a fly whisk, addressing two kneeling men. Below him are two Jaina monks, one seated on a stool, the other on a rug spread on the floor. They are also addressing the congregation consisting of men, women, and children, among whom is a Jaina nun dressed in white. Red background.

Vijñaptipatras are letters, usually in a scroll, containing an invitation from the Jaina community to a monk inviting him to spend the *paryushṇā* season with them. These letters were often illustrated with events of significance in the community issuing the invitation and also with portraits of the personages invited.

Nagaur, a fief of Marwar and a city of considerable antiquity, appears to have developed a variation of the Marwar style, at least towards the middle of the eighteenth century. Around this time, the chief of Nagaur, Bakht Singh, closely related to the ruling house, seized Jodhpur resulting in a partition of the state. The house of Bakht Singh ultimately prevailed and Marwar was reunited in 1772 under Vijay Singh, his son and successor.

148

149.

Rāginī Kakubh: illustration
from a *Rāgamālā* series
Marwar, late eighteenth century
$7\frac{7}{8} \times 5\frac{1}{4}$ inches

A lady, wearing a brimmed cap adorned with floral garlands and holding garlands in both hands, is flanked by a pair of peacocks on each side. Rows of floral plants in the foreground, sky with birds on top.

Above is a Brajbhāshā verse giving the iconographical form of the mode. It is written in white ink on a black ground.

150.

Rāginī Gauḍamalhār
Marwar, late eighteenth century
$3\frac{7}{8} \times 3\frac{5}{8}$ inches

A lady, seated on a pink rocky eminence in the center of a lake, plays on a *vīṇā*. Hills with palaces and trees in the background.

151.

Portrait of Mahārājā Bhīm Singh (1793–1803) of Jodhpur
Marwar, late eighteenth century
$8\frac{1}{4} \times 5\frac{3}{8}$ inches

Bhīm Singh, quite stiffly and awkwardly posed, rests one hand on a shield, the other on a poignard tucked into his belt.

His rule was a time of internecine quarrels and endless struggles with the Marathas.

152.

Equestrian portrait of Rao Rājā Buddh Singh of Bundi
Marwar, late eighteenth century
$11\frac{1}{8} \times 9\frac{1}{2}$ inches

The king, mounted on a large horse, smokes a *hukkā* carried by a footman. Other retainers carry the regalia including a staff, fly whisks, and a sunshade.

Buddh Singh ruled Bundi from 1695 to 1729. The Devanāgarī inscription *rāvrājā buddhsinhjī* is modern, but the identification is correct.

153.

Rāma's army: folio from a Ms. of the *Rāmāyaṇa*
Probably Marwar, early nineteenth century
$3\frac{1}{8} \times 7\frac{5}{8}$ inches

Rāma and Lakshmaṇa, accompanied by bears and monkeys armed with trees and branches, march in double file against the enemy.

154.

The summer season
Marwar, c. 1825
$14 \times 9\frac{3}{4}$ inches

The king, to be identified with Mān Singh of Marwar (1803–1843), is seated in a pavilion with thatch roof located next to a pool with numerous fountains. He is attended by a group of women, most of them cooling him with gentle breezes stirred by hand fans. Beyond the dark, cool foliage of the trees is the blazing and desolate landscape of summer, with bare hills and valleys scorched by a large golden sun.

155.

Princess seated by a window
Marwar, c. 1825
$5\frac{5}{8} \times 3\frac{5}{8}$ inches

The lady, with nimbus, leans against a crimson cushion placed against a bolster. The large eyes curving at the top and the pointed nose and chin are characteristic of the emphatically stylized figures of this period.

156.

Lady beneath a tree
Marwar, c. 1825
6×4 inches

The lady, with hands held above the head, fingers intercrossed, has slipped one foot out of her shoes and raises it above the ground as if it were pierced by a thorn. A crane with sharply pointed beak looks up at her.

The strong color, marked stylization and pronounced rhythms of this painting are characteristic of Marwar painting for the greater part of the nineteenth century.

154

Rājasthānī Style: Sirohi

The existence of a school in the state of Sirohi, which lies to the west of Mewar and to the south of Marwar, is being gradually recognized with the increasing availability of illustrated manuscripts and painted letters-of-invitation issued by the local Jaina community. Not unexpectedly, the school shares features derived from both Mewar and Marwar, but tends to be more conservative than either.

157.

Three folios from a Ms. of
the *Devī Mahātmya*
Probably Sirohi,
late eighteenth century
$4\frac{1}{2} \times 4$ inches

folio 9 obverse
The king on horseback.
folio 11 obverse
A merchant seated alone in the forest.
folio 11 reverse
The king and the merchant in conversation.
folio 46 reverse
The worship of Bhairavī.

The heavy color is associated with Sirohi work of the late eighteenth century.

Rājasthānī Style: Kishangarh

Like the school of Bikaner, the Kishangarh school was greatly influenced by the Mughal style. But it is imbued with a deeply felt religious fervor and a romantic lyricism combined with a refined technique derived from the later Mughal school which makes it unique. Building upon the kind of work patronized at the court of the Mughal emperor, Muhammad Shāh (1719–1748), it immediately discarded its heavy and empty sensuousness for a mood of exalted mysticism (Cat. no. 160). This change appears to have been due to Sāvant Singh, a great devotee of Kṛishṇa and famous as a poet under the name of Nāgarīdās. Sāvant Singh had a checkered political career, ruling haphazardly over a partitioned kingdom from the city of Rūpnagar from 1748 to 1764, during which he spent a great deal of time at Brindāban, the earthly playground of his Lord, Kṛishṇa. He was himself trained in painting and, as a patron, his influence upon the work of the period, particularly the master Nihāl Chand, must have been considerable. The exalted mood initiated during his reign was difficult to maintain, and the deep religious spirit that once informed the art having departed, the painting became merely decorative and pretty. Nevertheless, the Kishangarh school continued to produce fairly attractive works right up to the middle of the nineteenth century.

REFERENCES:

E. DICKINSON and K. KHANDALAVALA, *Kishangarh Painting*, (New Delhi, 1959).

158.

A musical entertainment
Kishangarh, c. 1735
$9\frac{1}{8} \times 6\frac{5}{8}$ inches

In the moonlit night, a princess, seated on a terrace by a pond, listens to two female musicians. Her posture is relaxed but attentive, the hands crossed over the chest. She is accompanied by a confidante holding a cup and an attendant who brings in a tray filled with jars and bottles. A full moon is in the sky, its reflection being visible in the pool behind the princess.

The color, architectural setting, and the stylized faces carry more than a hint of the familiar Kishangarh style of the mid-eighteenth century that was soon to follow.

In date, the painting is not far removed from Dickinson and Khandalavala, *Kishangarh Painting*, pl. II, which is assigned by the authors to c. 1739.

159.

The festival of Dīvālī
Kishangarh,
mid-eighteenth century
4 × 6 inches

A lady, dressed in red and yellowish green, holds a sparkler over the parapet of a terrace. Other fireworks blaze in the dark gray night.

The picture is a fragment of an originally much larger composition like the one reproduced by Dickinson and Khandalavala, *Kishangarh Painting*, pl. XI.

160.

Ladies in a landscape
Kishangarh,
mid-eighteenth century
$8\frac{5}{8} \times 12$ inches

In the foreground are a group of six women, the central figure offering what appears to be a tuft of grass to a friend who turns around to receive it. The latter is preceded by two companions, one of them balancing three milk pots on her head. In the rear of the group are two more women, one of them looking back into the distance.

The yellowish-green ground is bordered by a river that branches off to the right in order to form an island. On the bank are to be seen, from right to left, a prancing horse, a horse and an elephant, and several groups of women, some of whom are dressing themselves after a bath. To the left is a palace by a lake with two large boats; on the banks of the lake are two women.

On the river, in the background, is a large red boat; on the farther shore are hunters on elephants pursuing a rhinoceros, a kneeling elephant, groups of hunters, ox-drawn chariots, and elephants with pennants fluttering.

The figures, ethereal and unsubstantial

in nature, and sunk in deep reverie, endow the painting with an unreal, dreamlike atmosphere that is hauntingly evocative.

160

161.

The image of Śrī Nāthajī
Kishangarh,
mid-eighteenth century
$6\frac{1}{2} \times 4\frac{3}{4}$ inches

The image, dressed in a white *jāmā*, is drawn against a splash of bright red. An elaborate carpet in black and gold is placed before the image. The circular objects on both sides of the feet are bolsters. The bright red margin is painted with lotus arabesques in gold.

The rulers of Kishangarh were devout followers of the Vallabha cult, and like many rulers of Rajasthan, were devotees of the image of Śrī Nāthadvārā. Pictorial representations of the image were generally painted at the pilgrim center and carried back by those who visited there. This particular example was done at Kishangarh itself in the local style.

162.

A seated prince
Kishangarh,
late eighteenth century
$4 \times 2\frac{1}{2}$ inches

The prince, wearing a pink turban, is seated in the Persian fashion. He holds a

161

shield, while his sword rests on the ground. The painting is unfinished.

163.

Rādhā and Kṛishṇa
Kishangarh,
late eighteenth century
$8\frac{1}{2} \times 6$ inches

The God gently touches Rādhā below the chin. A tree is outlined in the background. The painting is unfinished.

164.

A lady on horseback
Kishangarh,
late eighteenth century
$5\frac{1}{4} \times 5\frac{7}{8}$ inches

The figures are outlined in black, so that the effect is that of a drawing enlivened with touches of color.

165.

Portrait of a Rajput chief
Kishangarh,
late eighteenth century
$7\frac{3}{8} \times 5$ inches

165

The chief, dressed in greenish-yellow *jāmā*, holds a sword with red scabbard in one hand and a lotus bud in the other. Rows of pearl garlands adorn his neck. Gray background.

The person represented may be Sawāī Pratāp Singh of Jaipur (1778–1803).

166.

Kṛishṇa sheltering Rādhā
Kishangarh,
end of the eighteenth century
$4\frac{3}{4} \times 3\frac{1}{8}$ inches

Against a dense row of plantains, the leaves of which are closed, stand Kṛishṇa and Rādhā. Kṛishṇa holds a bunch of lotuses thrown over his shoulder in one hand, while with the other he protectively stretches out an end of his scarf over Rādhā. In the foreground is a lotus pond.

The drawing is bold, departing from the conventional delicacy of Kishangarh work, giving the picture a somewhat unexpected vitality.

166

167.

Rādhā and Kṛishṇa
seated by the river
Kishangarh,
early nineteenth century
$5\frac{1}{2} \times 3\frac{3}{8}$ inches

The divine couple are shown seated on a chair placed atop a lotus. In the river are bathing elephants and a palatial building with steps leading to the water.

The painting is unfinished. The extreme stylization of the figures, the coarse shading of the faces, and the weak drawing indicate a period of decline.

168.

A Rajput prince
seated on a terrace
Kishangarh,
mid-nineteenth century
$9\frac{1}{8} \times 7$ inches

A prince, with nimbus, holds a betel leaf in one hand and converses with a man seated opposite. Behind him is an attendant waving a fly whisk of peacock feathers. Green ground, blue sky.

Towards the top of the green ground, in microscopic letters is the inscription: *amal nihāl chand krasangaḍh 1891 phagan*

168

badī . . . (The work of Nihāl Chand. Kishangarh, V.S. 1891/A.D. 1834 the month of Phālgun . . .).

If the ascription is genuine, it is certainly some Nihāl Chand other than the famous painter who worked at Kishangarh almost a hundred years earlier. The style of the painting is consistent with a mid-nineteenth century date.

169.

Portrait of a prince
Kishangarh,
mid-nineteenth century
$5 \times 3\frac{1}{2}$ inches

The prince, dressed in white, is seated by an arched window. He holds a book, and leans against a pink bolster. The facial features are frozen in what almost amounts to a caricature of Kishangarh conventions.

170.

Folio from an
unidentified romance
Kishangarh,
mid-nineteenth century
$5\frac{1}{2} \times 8\frac{5}{8}$ inches

On the obverse are three panels in which are placed a woman playing with a child; two hunters, one of whom is shooting an arrow; and, in the third panel, the same hunter performing penance with hands upraised, his weapons placed on the ground.

On the reverse is a panel showing two women, one of them eating from a large dish. The figures are angular and the colors strong, particularly the acid green of the background.

171.

The elopement
Probably Kishangarh,
dated V.S. 1922/A.D. 1865
$12\frac{1}{4} \times 7\frac{1}{4}$ inches

The lover ascends a ladder to reach the balcony where he is awaited by his beloved, the guards apparently being unaware of his presence. In the background is a rider on horseback leaping through space.

The colored drawing, done in a folk style with squat, dumpy figures, is pricked in order to serve as a stencil for other paintings.

सकरत कल समय प्रात रिन का निसप ति इत्त नेस पटक लस नीर आ
नत स प्रेम इ क दिवस आइरं घर बराज सुरसरित निबि धि क न्या स मा
ज ति हि गोंम इ रस माली प्रसिध संउत बिलस सुख स कल सिध बंधो
नगगब जित्र निविक अप छ रा कर तना टक अनेक अवगाह गंगा त
ल अंग अंगा मिलि कर त मनदु क्रीड़ा मतंग इहि समय रेनुका नीर आ

Rājasthānī Style: Bikaner

Of all the schools of Rajasthan, that of Bikaner seems to have been most closely affected by Mughal painting. The earliest works, dated to the middle of the seventeenth century, were painted by Mughal masters such as Alī Razā, who came to Bikaner from Delhi. Their descendants continued to work in this manner well into the eighteenth century but were increasingly influenced by the Rājasthānī environment. In contrast to the other schools, the names of several Bikaner painters have come down to us, the most notable among them being Ruknuddīn who achieved much fame and distinction. A painting by his son Ibrāhīm is in the Watson collection (Cat. no. 172). Toward the closing years of the eighteenth century, Bikaner work was increasingly assimilated into the more orthodox Rājasthānī manner, but continued to preserve a comparative delicacy of line and color (Cat. no. 184).

REFERENCES:
Khajanchi Catalogue, pp. 18–21, 48–55.
H. GOETZ, *The Art and Architecture of Bikaner* (Oxford, 1950).

172.

Kṛishṇa waking the sleeping Rādhā: folio from a series illustrating the *Rasikapriyā* of Keśavadāsa
Bikaner, dated V.S. 1748/A.D. 1691
$7\frac{3}{4} \times 5$ inches

An attendant converses with Kṛishṇa who is seated beneath a tree. We see him holding the hands of the sleeping Rādhā. An attendant is seated nearby, while two ascetics offer oblation to a sacrificial fire in the foreground.

The inscription on the reverse reads: *an° 29 jo° 86 kām vrihma ro sam° 1748* (Number 29, album 86, the work of Ibrāhīm, V.S. 1748/A.D. 1691).

Ibrāhīm was the son of the famous Ruknuddīn. A portrait of the painter is reproduced in the *Khajanchi Catalogue*, no. 115, Fig. 84. The strong color, particularly the bright yellow of the walls of the room and the bluish-green ground, is not quite the palette one would expect of a Bikaner artist of this period.

Another painting by Ibrāhīm is mentioned in the *Khajanchi Catalogue*, no. 91, and is dated A.D. 1685.

173.

A lady at worship
Bikaner, c. 1690
$5\frac{5}{8} \times 3\frac{1}{8}$ inches

A lady worships a Liṅga placed beneath a tree. The ritual water with which the Liṅga is lustrated drains into a pool which is bordered by tufts of grass. Softly painted ground, blue sky.

The painting is a product of the school of Ruknuddīn which flourished in the last quarter of the seventeenth century.

Cf. *Khajanchi Catalogue*, no. 89, Fig. 70.

172

174.

Lady and tree
Bikaner,
late seventeenth century
$4\frac{5}{8} \times 2\frac{1}{2}$ inches

The lady, dressed in a tunic reaching to the ankles and a golden crown, sits on the lowermost branch of a kumquat bush, holding on to one of its twigs. Birds can be seen resting on its branches and also on the ground; a pair of birds hover above the ground to the right. The light green ground merges into the soft gray sky in which are depicted rows of birds in flight. Cf. Cat. no. 175.

This motif was popular in Bikaner. For a later version see *Khajanchi Catalogue*, no. 99, Fig. 77.

175.

Lady and tree
Bikaner,
late seventeenth century
$4\frac{1}{2} \times 2$ inches

The painting is another version of Cat. no. 174, the line here being firmer and the colors a little bolder. We see also a conventional water pond in the foreground, and the hair of the lady flies out

174

175

in the breeze. Heavy clouds float in the sky, against which fly conventional rows of birds.

176–177.

Two paintings from
a *Rāgamālā* series
Bikaner, c. 1700
$5\frac{7}{8} \times 4\frac{1}{8}$ inches

(176.) Rāginī Vangāla
A man seated on a low stool is performing worship, scattering flower petals with one hand and holding a rosary with the other. In front of him is a mango tree, and behind him is a domed building with a leopard in the doorway. Pale apple-green ground.

The inscription on the reverse reads: *17 bangālo* (Rāginī Vangāla, no. 17).

(177.) Rāginī Gauḍa-Malhār
A man, feet crossed, is seated on lotus petals, resting one hand on a crutch, the other holding a string of beads. He wears a tiger-skin skirt, the torso being bare except for pearls and gems. The light gray ground culminates in a pink hill topped by buildings. A lotus pool is in the foreground.

The inscription on the reverse reads: *28 goḍ malhār* (Rāginī Gauḍa-Malhār, no. 28).

176

178.

A lady adjusting her veil
Bikaner, early eighteenth century
$6\frac{3}{4} \times 5\frac{1}{8}$ inches

The slender lady, with long legs and short torso, is simply dressed and gently tugs at the loose end of her sari which is pulled over her head to form a veil. Apple-green ground.

179.

The Rāsa-maṇḍala
Bikaner,
early eighteenth century
$6\frac{1}{8} \times 8\frac{3}{8}$ inches

In the center of the circle is Kṛishṇa, knees flexed in a dance pose, and holding a flute. He is surrounded by a group of musicians, singing and dancing, two on the top sprinkling him with colored water. Outside the circle are clumps of trees, with Nanda and Yaśodā on the left.

179

180.

The child Kṛishṇa
playing with his mother
Bikaner, early
eighteenth century
$9\frac{3}{4} \times 7$ inches

On the terrace of a palace is Yaśodā holding a scraggly but bejewelled Kṛishṇa by the hand. On both sides of her are attendants carrying regalia and an assortment of toys. On the upper floor of the palace is Nanda, flanked by attendants on either side, receiving the homage of a courtier.

181.

Rāginī Rāmakarī
Bikaner, early eighteenth century
$6\frac{1}{8} \times 3\frac{7}{8}$ inches

The angry heroine turns her face away from her lover, who touches her feet in order to assuage her anger. It is a dark night, only the crescent moon being visible. Attendants doze in the palace, the darkness being broken by flaming candles on the terrace. Cf. Cat. no. 32.

180

182.

Rāginī Ṭodī
Bikaner, mid-eighteenth century
$5 \times 3\frac{1}{2}$ inches

The lady leans against a mauve bolster, holding a *vīṇā* and a flower. A deer listens in rapt attention. Trees interspersed with cypresses in the background. Stylized clouds in the blue sky. Devanāgarī inscription on the reverse: *kām nāthū āmadjī ro* (the work of Nāthū Ahmad).

183.

Rāga Mālkauns
Bikaner, late eighteenth century
$11\frac{1}{4} \times 8$ inches

A man, seated on a throne, listens to musicians playing on a *tānpūrā* and a drum. A fountain in the foreground, a hall with gray walls, indicating night, in the background; a row of trees behind the walls.

Inscription on the reverse: *dusrau rāga mālakāns* (the second Rāga, Mālkauns).

183

184.

Princess and bird
Bikaner, late eighteenth century
$6\frac{1}{2} \times 4\frac{1}{2}$ inches

The princess, dressed in dark tunic and felt cap, stands in a gracefully arched balcony, a bird perched on the right hand. The walls are a pale ochre, and have tall narrow windows.

185.

A foreign lady
Probably Bikaner,
late eighteenth century
$7\frac{5}{8} \times 4\frac{3}{4}$ inches

The lady wears a pink hat and elaborate Indian jewelry, her hair done in loose curls that fall over her shoulders. A bird is perched on the right hand, the left holds a bunch of grapes.

184

185

Rājasthānī Style: Ajmer

A Rājasthānī school, the existence of which has only recently gained general recognition, is that of Ajmer, chiefly associated with the rulers of Sawar. It possesses distinctive stylistic characteristics, notably in the conscious use of unpainted areas, a technique derived no doubt from the Mughal *nīm qalam*. The contrast between the unpainted area and the rest of the painting, unlike Mughal painting, is enlivened by a use of bright and vivid accents of color. The school seems to owe much to the Bundi school, but is nevertheless distinctive.

186.

Two ladies at play
Ajmer, early eighteenth century
$6 \times 3\frac{5}{8}$ inches

The ladies hold each other's hands, palms upward, ready to swing and turn in play. The motif becomes popular in Indian painting from the early eighteenth century, late Mughal, Pahāṛī, and Rājasthānī examples being quite commonly found. One of the ladies is fair and wears Hindu dress; the other is attired in *pāi jāmā*, *jāmā*, and a *dupaṭṭā* crossed over the chest and fluttering over the shoulder. Color is applied only on the figures, the rest of the paper being left unpainted. A boldly written inscription in Devanagari at the top reads: *doya pāturkī he kudī deve* (a picture of two courtesans, they are hopping).

187.

Kṛishṇa leading Rādhā
through a garden
Ajmer, early eighteenth century
$9\frac{7}{8} \times 5\frac{1}{2}$ inches

Rādhā, holding Kṛishṇa by the hand, steps over a rough pebble-strewn path. The garden is indicated by ornamentally treated floral plants placed in horizontal rows. In the foreground are blossoming lotuses rising out of a pond; in the background is a row of plantains, one of which is in flower, alternating with other trees.

As in Cat. no. 186, the application of color is minimal, the ground being left unpainted. Hindi verse on top.

187

188.

Portrait of a bearded nobleman
Probably Ajmer,
early eighteenth century
$9\frac{1}{2} \times 4\frac{1}{2}$ inches

The prince is shown in an arched window holding a flower and a string of beads. A fountain in the foreground.

Rājasthānī Style: Jaipur (Amber)

Until recently little was known about painting in the state of Jaipur, traditionally called Amber, except for the work produced there in the eighteenth and nineteenth centuries. This was particularly surprising in view of the strength and fame of its rulers, who were the principal Rajput allies of the Mughals during the sixteenth and seventeenth centuries. New material (particularly a *Yaśodhara-charitra* painted at Amber in 1590 and a *Mahāpurāṇa* painted at Muazzamabad in 1606 together with the wall paintings at Bairat) reveal that the Amber style of the early seventeenth century, in spite of the close Mughal alliance, was hardly different from that of the other contemporary Rajput schools. There is a gap in our knowledge for most of the seventeenth century, but several series illustrating the *Rāgamālā*, previously considered to belong to Central India or Bikaner, can now be definitely assigned to the reign of the great Sawāī Jai Singh (1700–1743), a mathematician, astronomer and patron of learning and the arts. A rather stiff and formal style continued to flourish under his successors. But a dazzling, brilliant style was achieved during the reign of Sawāī Pratāp Singh (1778–1803), a brave soldier against overwhelming odds, devout worshipper of Govindjī, poet of considerable achievement (under the name of Brajanidhi), and fine musician and dancer. The entire nineteenth century was a period of great productivity, and though little of quality was produced, Jaipur paintings were exported all over North India. The Jaipur style was also quite hardy, and was among the last of the traditional styles to succumb to the pressure of changing times.

189.

Rāginī Āsāvarī
Probably Jaipur,
early eighteenth century
$8\frac{5}{8} \times 7$ inches

A lady, seated on a mound of earth symbolically representing a mountain, is shown holding a snake. In front of her is a musician, dressed in clothes made of rags sewn together, attracting snakes by playing on an *algojā* (a gourd pipe). Snakes are also seen clinging to the trunks of the surrounding trees.

190.

Rāginī Dhanāśrī
Probably Jaipur, first half
of the eighteenth century
$8\frac{1}{2} \times 7$ inches

A lady seated in a palace is shown painting a portrait of her beloved, who is riding out to meet her.

The verse written on top is by the poet Govinda. A *Rāgamālā* series from Malpura in Jaipur State, dated A.D. 1786, also illustrates a verse by the same poet (*Binney Catalogue*, no. 36).

191.

Rāginī Rāmakalī
Probably Jaipur, first half
of the eighteenth century
9×6 inches

The heroine petulantly turns away from her lover, who attempts to pacify her. The groom and the horse wait in the foreground. Elaborate architectural setting with rows of flowers.

A Brajabhāshā verse at the top gives the iconographical form of the musical mode.

192.

Rāga Hinḍol
Probably Jaipur, first half
of the eighteenth century
$7\frac{1}{4} \times 6$ inches

Kṛishṇa and Rādhā are seated on a swing which is rocked by two attendants. Others play on musical instruments, and two women are dancing. A lotus lake is in the foreground. The sky is filled with flashes of lightning. Two *apsarases* emerge from the clouds, one of them playing on a *tānpūrā*, the other showering flowers.

Brajabhāshā verse giving the iconographical form of the musical mode on the top.

193.

Mahārājā Sawāī Pṛithvī Singh
(1768–1778) of Jaipur
Jaipur, c. 1775
$6\frac{1}{4} \times 3\frac{7}{8}$ inches

Pṛithvī Singh, the son of Mādho Singh, was born in 1763 and ascended the throne when he was but five years of age. He died in 1778 at the age of fifteen.

192

194.

The month of Śrāvaṇa: illustration to the *Kavipriyā* of Keśavadāsa
Jaipur, c. 1786
6 × 4¾ inches

It is the rainy season—lightning flashes in the clouds and peacocks cry from the trees. In the foreground are three rivers flowing into the sea. In a pavilion are the hero and the heroine, conversing.

The verse from Keśavadāsa is superscribed on top; see *Keśava Granthāvalī*, p. 158.

No. 36, *Binney Catalogue*, is a reproduction of a painting from a *Rāgamālā* series reputedly painted by the artist Rāmkishan at Malpura and dated A.D. 1786. If this information is correct, the painting under discussion here is close enough in style to be of about the same date and by the same artist.

Malpura is not a *ṭhikānā*, but a city 55 miles south of Jaipur, roughly midway between Jaipur and Bundi. It was the most important commercial center of the state at least until the nineteenth century and was directly under the Jaipur kings.

194

195–196.

Two paintings from
a *Rāgamālā* series
Jaipur, c. 1825
$5\frac{1}{8} \times 3\frac{7}{8}$ inches

(195.) Rāga Dīpak
Rādhā and Kṛishṇa are seated on a couch, Kṛishṇa holding a mirror. In front of them are two female musicians, one of them playing a drum. Candles light up the terrace.

Brajabhāshā verse on top.

(196.) Rāga Megha Malhār
Kṛishṇa, holding a flute in his raised hand, dances to the music played by four *gopīs*.

Brajabhāshā verse on top.

197.

Lady on a terrace
smoking a *hukkā*
Jaipur, c. 1825
$4\frac{3}{4} \times 2\frac{7}{8}$ inches

The painting is reminiscent of contemporary work from Marwar.

198.

The image of
Govindadeva-jī at Galta
Jaipur, mid-nineteenth century
$6\frac{1}{4} \times 5$ inches

Next to the image of Kṛishṇa holding a flute is the image of his consort. Attendants, holding boxes on trays, stand on both sides. Ritual utensils are placed on low stools in front of the image.

199.

Rāma and Sītā enthroned
Jaipur, mid-nineteenth century
$7\frac{1}{8} \times 9\frac{3}{8}$ inches

Hanumān, the monkey general, presses the feet of Rāma as an act of devotion, while Lakshmaṇa waves a peacock-feather fly whisk. Beyond the lotus lake is the city of Ayodhyā.

200.

Kṛishṇa and Rādhā in a swing
Jaipur, late nineteenth century
$17\frac{3}{8} \times 14\frac{5}{8}$ inches

This hastily painted picture, using crude aniline dyes, is an example of the vain effort by traditional artists to compete with the cheap, painted oleographs which were beginning to flood the markets and threaten their living.

201.

Śiva seated on an elephant skin
Jaipur, early twentieth century
$3\frac{1}{8} \times 8\frac{1}{8}$ inches

Pictures of this type mark the last phase of traditional painting in India. Workmanship in this style continues to the present day, and is often reproduced in the numerous wall calendars and mounted pictures sold in the bazaars of north Indian cities.

Rājasthānī Style: Bundelkhand

With the accession to power of Bīr Singh Dev of Orchha (c. 1605–1627), a particular favorite of the Emperor Jahāngīr, great architectural plans were set in motion, and the splendid palaces at Orchha and Datia were the result. The state of the painter's art at this time is not clearly known, but judging from the fragments of wall paintings that survive, it seems to have been a provincial version of the Mughal style. Examples of painting from this region are again known from the late eighteenth century onwards and represent yet another local expression of the Rājasthānī style.

REFERENCE:

N.C. MEHTA, *Studies in Indian Painting* (Bombay, 1926).

202–203.

Two miniatures from a series illustrating the verse of Matirām
Bundelkhand,
late eighteenth century
$9 \times 7\frac{1}{4}$ inches

(202.) A lady waiting for her lover.
The lady, waiting for her lover, is seated in an enclosed courtyard outside a pavilion in which is an empty bed. Two friends discuss her emotional state. Outside, in another pavilion, is the absent lover smoking a *hukkā*. The long, pleated *jāmā* and flat turban are characteristic features of dress in painting of this period, particularly from Datia. Gardens and groves are indicated by rows of trees.

N.C. Mehta first published paintings of this style in his pioneering *Studies in Indian Painting*. Several miniatures of the style reached the market in the 1950's after the dispersal of the collections of the erstwhile Datia state.

The Brajabhāshā couplet which forms the subject matter of this painting is inscribed at the top.

(203.) A lady waiting for her lover by the riverside: illustration to a verse by the poet Matirām.
Bees hover over the row of trees in the background. Among the rocks that border the river is a fish, and to the lady's right are two birds. Her eyes are compared to all of these—bees, fish and birds—as they look out expectantly for the lover's arrival. In the foreground are two women in conversation, one of them pointing towards the lady.

At the top is the Brajabhāshā verse by Matirām.

203

204.

Portrait of Rāo Śatrujit
(1762–1801) of Datia
Bundelkhand,
late eighteenth century
$7\frac{5}{8} \times 5\frac{5}{8}$ inches

The king, his hand resting on a sword, is dressed in a *jāmā* reaching to the ankles. He wears a yellow turban, and a bright yellow shawl is loosely wound around the waist. He holds a rose.

A Devanāgarī inscription on the reverse identifies the king:

śrī mahārājādhirāj śrī mahārāja śrī
rāu rājā satrajit bahādur jū deva

205–206.

Two paintings from a series illustrating the *Satsaī* of Bihārī
Bundelkhand,
late eighteenth century
$6\frac{7}{8} \times 7\frac{7}{8}$ inches

(205.) The *nāyaka* (hero), with a female attendant, discusses the beauty of the *nāyikā* (heroine) as they stand in a rose garden.

Brajabhāshā verse on the reverse.

(206.) The situation is the same as in Cat. no. 205, except that the *nāyaka* is shown in conversation with a male friend.

207.

A painting from a series illustrating the *Satsaī* of Bihārī
Bundelkhand,
late eighteenth century
$7 \times 7\frac{5}{8}$ inches

Two ladies, on a terrace in a garden, discuss the desolate state of the *nāyikā* who is separated from her beloved.

Brajabhāshā verse on top.

208.

Illustrated folio
from an unidentified work
by the poet Kṛishṇa
Bundelkhand,
late eighteenth century
$3\frac{3}{4} \times 3\frac{5}{8}$ inches

Obverse: Kṛishṇa, dressed in a bright yellow *dhotī* and carrying a golden staff, throws red colored powder at Rādhā. Green background. Pots and pools of red color on the ground.

Reverse: Kṛishṇa turns around to look at Rādhā, who has just thrown colored powder on him. Green ground with pots and a pool of color.

209.

An episode from the *Rāmāyaṇa*
Bundelkhand,
late eighteenth century
$6\frac{3}{4} \times 10\frac{1}{4}$ inches

Next to the golden city of Laṅkā, within an enclosure having pink walls and fortifications, are Rāma and Lakshmaṇa seated on a jewelled platform. One of the monkey chiefs has his hands folded in adoration, the other prostrates himself on the ground. A headless corpse, whose forearms are also missing, lies on the ground.

210.

The month of Agahan:
miniature from a *Bārāmāsā* series
Bundelkhand,
late eighteenth century
$6\frac{1}{4} \times 9\frac{7}{8}$ inches

The cold season is indicated by ascetics warming themselves before a fire, a man and woman bundled together in a blanket, and another couple warming their hands before a brazier. In the foreground, to the left, we see a lady conversing with her attendant. She is the target of the God of Love, who, concealed in a tree, aims a flowery arrow at her. To the right are the lovers dallying on an open terrace. Full moon with stars in the sky. River with lotus flowers in the foreground.

On the reverse are several Avadhī verses pertaining to the month and the season. There is also a stamp which says: *tasvīr khānā, datiā sṭeṭ, no. 5* (the Picture Gallery, Datia state, no. 5).

Rājasthānī Style: Various Schools

In spite of the great progress made in reconstructing the various schools of Rajasthan, there still remain behind many miniatures which it is not possible to assign definitely to any particular area or style. Some tentative suggestions can be made on the basis of stylistic similarities, but firm conclusions would be unreliable in the present state of our knowledge. It is best to wait for more evidence before a definite judgment can be made.

211.

Worship at a Kṛishṇa temple
Rājasthānī Style,
early eighteenth century
$14 \times 11\frac{7}{8}$ inches

Before an image of Kṛishṇa playing on the flute are arranged numerous offerings, including flowering plants and flower pots meant to represent a garden. In addition to the priest and his attendant there are several Rajput noblemen with hands folded in worship. The pillars and cusped arches are painted with delicately drawn but bright flowers.

211

The painting is related to work from the Ajmer-Merwara area and Bundi, and is possibly from the northern Mewar region.

212.

Ladies at their baths and
at leisure in a palace
Rājasthānī Style,
early eighteenth century
$11 \times 7\frac{7}{8}$ inches

On the open terrace of a palace is a pool in which several ladies are swimming, using large jars as floats. On the edge of the terrace, next to the flower beds, are two standing women, one of them carrying a pot. A lady having her body rubbed with oil, and another smoking a *hukkā* are at the back.

The workmanship is reminiscent of Bikaner work, though the draughtsmanship is not as delicate and the colors are brighter.

213.

An abbot at the window
Rājasthānī Style,
eighteenth century
$6\frac{1}{4} \times 4$ inches

213

Framed by an arched window is the portrait of a monk with a white beard and wearing a cowl. The hard outline of the halo and the beard, the eyes shaped like lotus petals, and the color, particularly the pink underside of the green cowl, establish the Rājasthānī origin of this miniature. It appears to have been inspired by a Mughal version of an engraving representing St. Anthony Abbot by Raphael Sadeler, after Martin de Vos. See Milo C. Beach "The Gulshan Album and its European Sources," Museum of Fine Arts, Boston, *Bulletin*, LXIII (1965, no. 332), p. 73, Figs. 4 and 4a.

Versions of Mughal paintings and European engravings dating to the mid- and late eighteenth century are known from Mewar, and it is possible that this example is of the Mewar school.

214.

Prince crossing a river
to meet his beloved
Rājasthānī Style,
mid-eighteenth century
$8\frac{3}{4} \times 6$ inches

The prince, on horseback, is fording a stream during the rainy season. His beloved waits for him in the balcony of a tower. A large boat in the foreground.

Stencils with color notes, like the present example, were used by artists for making copies.

215.

A Tīrthaṅkara renouncing
the world
Rājasthānī Style,
late eighteenth century
$3\frac{3}{4} \times 7\frac{1}{2}$ inches

To the right, outside a walled city, is the Tīrthaṅkara being carried, before the renunciation, in a procession on a palanquin. Ahead of him are flag-bearers, musicians, and a row of Gods, including Indra upon his elephant and the Sun God in his chariot. The Tīrthaṅkara is next seen seated beneath a tree. He has discarded his clothing and is cutting his hair.

On the reverse is a large flowering plant.

216.

A king smoking a *hukkā*
Rājasthānī Style,
late eighteenth century
$5\frac{1}{2} \times 8$ inches

A king, of advanced age and dressed in white, smokes a *hukkā* with an elaborately jewelled mouthpiece. He is attended by a *chaurī* bearer and by a seated figure with hands folded in a gesture of respect. Blue background.

The painting is reminiscent of late eighteenth-century work produced in Bundi and Kotah, and could be from that general area.

217.

A lacquered and
painted book cover
Rājasthānī Style,
late eighteenth century
$7 \times 4\frac{5}{8}$ inches

The decoration consists of an elephant formed by the intertwined bodies of women (*nārī-kuñjara*) with Kṛishṇa as the rider.

218.

A throne cover
Rājasthānī Style,
early nineteenth century
54×31 inches

The elaborately painted textile is accented with gold. A richly painted floral pattern consisting of lotus flowers, buds, and leaves occupies the central field. Above are conventional rocky shapes representing Mount Govardhana, on which stands Kṛishṇa as Śrī Nāthjī flanked by cowmaids. Of the two registers, the top one shows Śrī Nāthjī adored by female devotees carrying fly whisks and lamps on trays; the bottom one depicts a herd of cows attended by two cowherds.

Cloths of this type, used to cover thrones, are called *simhāsanas* (cf. Cat. no. 125). The workmanship is reminiscent of Sanganer, where painted cloths were manufactured in large quantities. The cover does not appear to be from the Deccan, especially not from Masulipatnam, which was the greatest center of the manufacture of painted cloths called *pintados*.

See John Irwin, "Golconda Cotton Painting of the Early Seventeenth Century," *Lalit Kalā*, 5 (April 1959), pp. 11–48.

219.

Ladies with a bird cage
Rājasthānī Style,
early nineteenth century
$3\frac{1}{2} \times 4\frac{1}{4}$ inches

This brightly painted page, showing a lady holding a cage with two birds, is probably a fragment of a folio from an illustrated manuscript of the *Yaśodhara-charitra*. The large eyes with upturned ends and the squat figures with large heads indicate a date in the nineteenth century. The color is reminiscent of work produced in Marwar, and more particularly Sirohi, in southern Rajasthan.

220.

Lady and deer
Rājasthānī Style,
early nineteenth century
$7\frac{1}{4} \times 4\frac{3}{8}$ inches

The lady, wearing a large turban, is shown playing on the lute to a black antelope. In the foreground are two rows of trees and a Śiva temple. The color and the stylized foliage of the trees are reminiscent of the Marwar and Sirohi styles.

221.

Four folios representing
the Jaina Tīrthaṅkaras
Rājasthānī Style,
late eighteenth century
$8\frac{3}{4} \times 3$ inches

Each folio is divided into six panels containing a crowned and throned Jaina accompanied by his emblem. Though the illustrations are of the late eighteenth century, the conventions followed are derived from the Western Indian style of the sixteenth century.

222.

Restraining runaway elephants
Rājasthānī Style,
mid-nineteenth century
$4\frac{3}{4} \times 5\frac{5}{8}$ inches

In the foreground are two runaway elephants, and attempts are being made by footmen to restrain them with fireworks. Above the small pool is yet another elephant, while a fourth elephant, ridden by a standard-bearer, is grappling with a tree trunk. Above is a city behind a hill, and a row of horsemen stretch from one end of the picture to the other.

223.

The secret meeting
Rājasthānī Style,
mid-nineteenth century
$11\frac{1}{4} \times 8\frac{7}{8}$ inches

The lover climbs up a knotted rope that has been let down by a maid, while the lady reclines on a bed on the terrace. It is a cloudy night with flashes of lightning; the guards doze at the gate of the palace and a horse and groom wait for the end of the tryst.

The painting is reminiscent of work at Alwar.

224.

Two folios from
an illustrated Ms. of *Chitrasena*
and *Ratanmañjarī*
Probably Rājasthānī Style,
nineteenth century
$6\frac{5}{8} \times 9\frac{1}{4}$ inches

Obverse: Ratanmañjarī requests Chitrasena, who is disguised as a Yogī, to recount the events leading to his renunciation.

Reverse: Ratanmañjarī carries food to Chitrasena who appears as a Yogī. The

foliage of the central tree is outlined by verses.

Obverse: The women of the harem dazzled by Chitrasena's beauty.

Reverse: Chitrasena being requested to abandon the mendicant's life and stay behind to enjoy a life of pleasure.
The verses are written both in Devanāgarī and Arabic script, and are sometimes fancifully arranged in the shape of trees and along the borders of the illustrations. The paintings are simple, possessing the naïve charm of folk art.

Basohli and Related Styles

The term "Basohli Style" is used here to designate a distinct group of paintings which were painted all over the Hill states, and not necessarily at Basohli itself. From the point of style, they share several broad features which are quite different from the Kangra style. The style seems to have come into existence towards the latter half of the seventeenth century and to have been gradually replaced by the Kangra style about the middle of the eighteenth century—although some work inspired by the Basohli style continued to be painted even later.

The application of the term "Basohli Style" may appear to be unusually broad, but is for the time being quite serviceable to understanding the early Pahāṛī style. This is true particularly since artists or their descendants were constantly moving from one Hill state to another, each of these states being of extremely small size. Fresh research by Mr. W.G. Archer and Dr. B.N. Goswamy, currently in progress, may throw new light on the variations of this idiom.

225.

Bāz-Bahādur and Rūpmatī
Basohli Style, c. 1700
$6\frac{1}{2} \times 6$ inches

The richly dressed lovers are shown riding gorgeously caparisoned horses. Rūpmatī turns around to look intently at her lover who holds a rose. The landscape is dark, the rows of trees along the rocky and curving horizons being painted in muted greens and blues. The white glistening bodies of the sarus cranes which flash out of the foliage indicate that it is the rainy season.

The picture has been badly soiled along the edges by moisture but is a fine example of its type. It is related to the workshop which produced "Rādhā and the pot," reproduced in K. Khandalavala, *Pahāṛī Miniature Painting*, Bombay, 1958, pl. C.

226.

Rājā Chhatar Singh
(1664–1690) of Chamba
Basohli Style (Chamba),
early eighteenth century
$6\frac{3}{8} \times 10\frac{1}{8}$ inches

The Rājā, dressed in red, holds prayer

beads in one hand and pours drink into a cup held by a kneeling attendant with the other. A servant holds a *hukkā*, ready to offer it to his master, while another attendant waves a fly whisk made of peacock feathers. Striped carpet, apple-green ground.

Several portraits of Chhatar Singh or Śatru Singh have survived. This miniature appears to have been painted shortly after the one reproduced by Khandalavala, *Pahāṛī Miniature Painting*, Fig. 63, correctly identified by B.N. Goswamy, *Roopa Lekha*, 35 (1966), p. 72, as representing Chhatar Singh in court. This miniature is possibly contemporary with the reign of the king.

225

226

227.

Portrait of a hill chief
Basohli Style,
early eighteenth century
$7\frac{1}{8} \times 5$ inches

The man, dressed in green except for a red *kamarband*, sits on a blue carpet decorated with red flowers. He holds a staff in one hand, while the other touches the hilt of a sword encased in a red scabbard. Deep yellow background.

228.

A lady braiding her hair
Basohli Style,
early eighteenth century
$6\frac{3}{4} \times 4\frac{3}{4}$ inches

The lady, kneeling opposite a mirror, is shown in the act of twisting three strands of hair at the back of her head. A cosmetic box lies on the yellow rug. Blue background with a strip of white indicating clouds towards the top.

227

229.

Lakshmī-Nārāyaṇa
Basohli Style, c. 1730
$7 \times 4\frac{7}{8}$ inches

The four-armed God is dressed in an orange *dhotī* spotted with gold, jewelry, and a three-peaked crown, the tips of which bear lotuses. He is seated on a large lotus which rises from a conventional lake, his consort seated on the lap. Yellow background, a strip of blue on the top.

230.

Rāginī Devagandhārī
Basohli Style, c. 1730
$6\frac{7}{8} \times 6\frac{7}{8}$ inches

A lady, accompanied by a maid who waves a fly whisk, offers worship to a Śiva Linga placed on a rather tall and elaborate pedestal. Blue sky with clouds on top.

The Ṭākrī inscription at the top reads: *rāganī devagandhārī malkose dī bhāryā gaur* (Rāginī Devagandhārī, wife of Rāga Malkauns, she is fair).

231

231.

Rājā Śamsher Sen
(1727–1781) of Mandi
Mandi, c. 1750
$6\frac{1}{4} \times 4\frac{7}{8}$ inches

The Rājā, whose hair is decorated with flowers and whose forehead is prominently marked with ashes, appears to be carrying an axe in the right hand. A black and white shawl covers his shoulders. Behind him is an attendant in white carrying a fly whisk of peacock feathers. Bluish-gray background, blue sky with clouds and conventional flocks of birds.

The Ṭākrī inscriptions, which have not been fully deciphered, identify the king. From other portraits (cf. R. Skelton *Indian Miniatures from the XVth to the XIXth Century*, Venice, 1961, pl. 53), he appears to have been a great devotee of Śiva, imitating in his daily action the life of his preferred God. The kingdom of Mandi appears to have been dedicated to Śiva, as the chief is constantly referred to as the Dīvān, a practice followed by several Indian rulers, notably Jaipur where Sawāī Pratāp Singh, after dedicating his kingdom to Govindjī, always referred to himself as Śrī Dīvān.

232.

Rāgaputra Kānarā
Pahāṛī Style, mid-eighteenth century
$8\frac{1}{4} \times 6$ inches

A musician, holding a lute, is accompanied by a man who keeps time by clapping his hands. The walls of the building are decorated with numerous niches, and the slender pavilions on the terrace project into the cloudy sky.

The painting belongs to a *Rāgamālā* series related to the Berlin *Rāgamālā* published in E. and Rose Leonore Waldschmidt, *Miniatures of Musical Inspiration*, Berlin, 1967. The workshop or the provenance cannot be determined exactly, though several features are derived from groups of painting collectively ascribed to the Basohli style.

233.

Portrait of Guru Haragovind
Pahāṛī Style,
mid-eighteenth century
$7\frac{1}{2} \times 5$ inches

The Guru, dressed in courtly fashion, wears a pink turban, white *jāmā*, and striped *pāi jāmā* cut away above the ankles. He holds a sword encased in a red scabbard. Dark olive-green ground.

The painting, in its coloring, appears to be related to a group of paintings generally associated with the early school of Kulu.

234.

Ladies under a tree
Pahāṛī Style, c. 1750–1775
$6\frac{1}{2} \times 4\frac{3}{8}$ inches

The ladies, one of them dressed in orange and yellow, the other in pink and white, hold on to the branches of a conventional tree as they engage in conversation. Bluish-gray background.

Paintings of this type, somewhat free and rough in execution, are generally thought to be folk productions. They seem to be related to some workshops that flourished at Mandi and Kulu.

235.

Indra, the king of the Gods
Pahāṛī Style, c. 1750–1775
$6\frac{1}{8} \times 5\frac{1}{2}$ inches

The white elephant, with a massive body and a small head, carries the God seated on a howdah, which tilts precariously over the elephant's neck. The attendant, kneeling behind, wears a *jāmā* spotted with leaves and is apparently flourishing a fly whisk.

This picture, like Cat. no. 234, is in a folk idiom related to work produced at Mandi and Kulu.

Kangra and Related Styles

The Kangra style, like the Basohli style, is a generic term used to describe a large group of paintings done in the various Hill states (including Basohli) possibly by a number of ateliers (*gharānās*). A curvilinear line, easy lyricism, and fluent movement distinguish paintings of the Kangra style, wherever they may have been painted, from the strong color and abstract statement of the Basohli style. Various Hill states in which the Kangra style flourished are known, but it is not clear if the differences are due to locality or to a particular atelier that happened to be there during a given time. Until a clearer understanding of these problems is achieved, the traditional classification and terminology will continue to be useful.

The Kangra style, understood as above, flourished roughly from the last quarter of the eighteenth century to the middle of the nineteenth century. It was adapted to some extent by the Sikh kingdom of the Punjab plains and certainly by governors and chiefs appointed by the Sikhs in the hills. The style continued to exist until the closing years of the nineteenth century, although the finest work was produced from c. 1780 to 1815.

236.

The daughter of Ugrasena
threatened with death
Kangra Style, c. 1780
$8\frac{3}{4} \times 12$ inches

A king, brandishing a sword, has jumped up on a chariot drawn by bullocks, and seized the woman who occupies it by the hair. The young man, who is riding alongside, seeks to protect her. The group of women behind the chariot are shown in various attitudes of amazement and dismay. Ahead of the cart are retainers, musicians on horseback, and standard-bearers. In the background is a large retinue with horsemen, elephants with covered howdahs, and soldiers.

The drawing is sensitive and probably belongs to the same atelier that produced the *Nala-Damayantī* drawings of the Boston Museum of Fine Arts. Cf. A.C. Eastman, *The Nala-Damayantī Drawings*, Boston, 1959.

237.

An illustration to
the *Gīta Govinda*
Kangra Style,
late eighteenth century
$7 \times 10\frac{1}{4}$ inches

This tracing of a painting from a *Gīta Govinda* series shows Rādhā, accompanied by an attendant and leaning against the branches of a leafless tree, as she searches for the absent Kṛishṇa.

238.

A hill chief
adoring the Goddess
Kangra Style,
late eighteenth century
$7\frac{5}{8} \times 4\frac{7}{8}$ inches

In a golden temple is shown the four-armed Goddess, holding a noose, an elephant goad, a bow, and arrows. She is seated on the recumbent Śiva, her spouse, who holds an hour-glass drum, the trident lying at the side. The Goddess has two female attendants who wave a fly whisk and a fan. Figures of Brahmā, Vishṇu, Śiva, and Indra (?), and a large pitcher are placed on the bright red carpet.

238

Outside the temple, to the left, is the king, praying; facing him is a seated female figure, perhaps the queen. The temple is placed in a grove of trees. A river flows in the foreground.

239.

Rājā Jagat Prakash
(c. 1770–1789) of Sirmur
Kangra Style,
late eighteenth century
$9\frac{7}{8} \times 7\frac{7}{8}$ inches

The Rājā, a large figure dressed in white, is among the crowds of Gods, ascetics, and monkey- and bear-kings who adore the enthroned Rāma and Sītā. The three brothers of Rāma are in attendance behind the throne. A priest raises his hands in laudatory song, and an ascetic has prostrated himself on the ground.

239

240.

Rājā Bīr Singh
(c. 1789–1846) of Nurpur
Kangra Style,
late eighteenth century
$7\frac{5}{8} \times 4\frac{5}{8}$ inches

The Rājā, shown in a window with cusped arches, wears a dark blue *jāmā* and a bright red shawl. He is attended by a retainer waving a fly whisk.

The features of the Rājā are clear, strong, and expressive. For another portrait see Khandalavala, *Pahāṛī Miniature Painting*, Study Supplement, Fig. no. 190.

241.

Nobleman on a terrace
Kangra Style,
late eighteenth century
$8 \times 5\frac{1}{4}$ inches

The aging nobleman, dressed in white, holds the stem of the *hukkā* in the left hand with a falcon perched on his gloved right hand. Beyond the terrace on which he is seated is a blue sky with clouds.

240

242.

Portrait of a hill Rājā
Kangra Style,
late eighteenth century
$5\frac{1}{4} \times 6\frac{3}{8}$ inches

A bearded king, attended by a *chaurī* bearer and a man holding a tray, is shown seated on an open terrace. Beyond the parapet are flowering plants.

243.

Portrait of a nobleman
Pahāṛī Style,
late eighteenth century
$6\frac{1}{8} \times 4\frac{1}{4}$ inches

The nobleman's simple white dress is relieved by a rich red shawl thrown loosely over the right shoulder. He wears elaborate Śaiva marks on the forehead and sandalwood paste across the throat. In his hands are what appear to be a *pān* leaf and a *pān* folded into a cone and ready for eating. Dark green background.

Traces of earlier eighteenth-century idioms survive in the color and in the strong and expressive face, but the picture has not escaped the impress of the graceful and lyrical work of the late eighteenth century.

243

244.

Rāga Vilāval
Pahāṛī Style,
late eighteenth century
$8\frac{1}{2} \times 5\frac{3}{8}$ inches

A man, leaning against a bolster, plays on the sarod. Facing him is a seated woman offering him *pān* from a tray. The buildings in the background project against a blue sky. The border is an unusual pink.

The picture retains early mannerisms, particularly in the handling of architectural elements, but the figures are entirely in the tradition of the late eighteenth century. It may be a late development of the kind of work represented by Cat. no. 232.

Devanāgarī inscription on the top margin:

Rāga Velāul Bhairo dā putra 14
(Rāga Vilāval, the son of Bhairava, no. 14).

245.

Rāginī Guṇakarī
Pahāṛī Style,
late eighteenth century
$8\frac{7}{8} \times 5\frac{1}{4}$ inches

244

Outside a pavilion equipped with a bed is a lady of rank, arranging flowers in a large pot and attended by a female *chaurī* bearer. In the foreground are ducks in a pond; in the background, three trees, one of them beyond the enclosure. Blue sky with white clouds.

The iconographical features of the Rāginī are those found in Rājasthānī examples. The warm coloring is also reminiscent of Rajasthan, but the female figures and the linear rhythms are unmistakably Pahāṛī.

246.

Adoration of Kṛishṇa
Kangra Style, c. 1800
$6\frac{1}{8} \times 7$ inches

The God, seated on a lotus, plays on a flute and gazes at the beloved Rādhā who is also seated on a lotus, hands folded in adoration. On both sides of the Divine Lovers are attendants carrying offerings, and worshipping cowherds. At the edge of the platform is another cowherd, bowing low, and in the foreground are cows and a calf.

The painting is unfinished.

247.

Love scene
Kangra Style, c. 1800
$8\frac{1}{4} \times 5\frac{1}{8}$ inches

The lovers are shown in a richly furnished room with a red carpet and a bed with embroidered pillows and bedspreads. The walls have niches and the door is panelled. The woman shyly covers the eyes of her lover as he seeks to embrace and undress her.

The gray walls and the candlestick on the carpet indicate night.

248.

Kṛishṇa sheltering
Rādhā from the rain
Kangra Style, c. 1800
$7\frac{1}{2} \times 4\frac{5}{8}$ inches

As clouds gather in the sky and it begins to rain, Kṛishṇa stretches out a black blanket to shelter Rādhā who runs towards him. The couple and a cow are shown beneath a tree from the foliage of which droop white flowers. The lower right corner is cut by a stream with delicate pink lotus blossoms and leaves. A calf bends down to drink the water.

249.

A hill Rājā holding court
Kangra Style,
end of eighteenth century
$8\frac{1}{2} \times 10\frac{7}{8}$ inches

All the figures are dressed in *bāsantī* (yellow-green), indicating that the occasion is the spring court. The rather stiff and halting workmanship indicates that the picture is a copy of an earlier painting of about the mid-eighteenth century.

250.

The transfer of babes
Kangra Style,
early nineteenth century
$11\frac{3}{4} \times 18\frac{7}{8}$ inches

To the left, within a prison with locked doors and sleeping guards, are shown Vasudeva and Devakī, the parents of Kṛishṇa. Subsequently, they adore the divine child in the form of Vishṇu seated on a lotus as Gods shower flowers from the sky. In the next scene, in the center of the miniature, the doors of the prison are miraculously opened, and in the foreground is Vasudeva, sheltered by the serpent Vasuki, crossing the river

247

Yamunā with the baby Kṛishṇa to reach the village of Gokul, the inhabitants of which are asleep. He exchanges Kṛishṇa for the daughter of Yaśodā (bottom right corner), returns with the baby girl to present it to Devakī (top right), the prison doors being again locked miraculously. The wicked Kaṁsa, accompanied by retainers (bottom left), is shown proceeding to the prison with the intention of slaying the child.

251.

An episode from the *Hamīr Haṭh*
Kangra Style,
early nineteenth century
$10\frac{3}{8} \times 13\frac{1}{2}$ inches

Sultān Alā-ud-dīn Khalji is shown on a hunt, accompanied by his women who carry spears. He pursues deer and aims an arrow at what appears to be a rat. To the right edge of the tent wall is Queen Murhathi, riding out on horseback. We next see her making love to a guard of the camp, Mahimā Sāh, who demonstrates his bravery by shooting a tiger without disengaging from the lady.

See Hirananda Sastri, "The Hamīr Haṭh or the Obstinacy of Hamīr," *Journal of Indian Art and Industry*, XVII, no. 132 (1916), pp. 35–40.

252.

Waiting for the lover
Kangra Style,
early nineteenth century
$8\frac{3}{4} \times 6\frac{1}{2}$ inches

On the terrace of a building is a pensive woman conversing with a confidante who holds her by the hem of her shawl. Dark clouds, lit up by flashes of serpentine lightning, fill the night sky and pour rain upon the distant landscape.

Behind the lady is a room with an empty bed and a lantern.

253.

The descent of the Ganges
Kangra Style,
early nineteenth century
9×6 inches

Śiva, accompanied by Pārvatī, is seated on a tiger skin in a cave surrounded by pink crags. They are accompanied by the bull Nandi. From Śiva's matted locks springs a stream of water which is received by an ascetic. He is apparently Bhagīratha, who practices penance on one foot in order to persuade the River Goddess to descend to earth to purify the remains of his ancestors.

253

The mountains are bare except for two pairs of birds sheltering in nooks, and three trees.

254.

A pensive lady
listening to music
Kangra Style,
early nineteenth century
$8\frac{1}{2} \times 5\frac{1}{4}$ inches

A princess, with hair falling loosely over the shoulder, leans over a bolster placed on an ornate chair. She is lost in thought, absently holding the end of the *hukkā* pipe in her hands. Facing her are two attendants, one of them holding a sun-shade, the other playing on a *tānpūrā*. Behind her are two more attendants in concerned conversation, one of them holding a tray with a box. All are dressed in white or light pink. The river swirls below and on the opposite bank are fields and houses.

255.

A lady meets her lover
Kangra Style,
early nineteenth century
$8\frac{7}{8} \times 6\frac{1}{2}$ inches

254

The elaborately canopied bed is set next to a fountain and flower beds. The lady approaches her lover, who is seated on the bed, her head bent shyly. Beyond the enclosure wall are trees, a river with a boat, and a hilly landscape.

256.

A wooden book cover
Kangra Style,
early nineteenth century
$7\frac{7}{8} \times 12\frac{3}{8}$ inches

On the obverse, the Goddess rides a tiger, holding a trident, a sword, a bowl, and a shield in each of her four hands; on the reverse is the monkey-chief Hanumān flying through the air. He carries a mountain in one hand and flourishes a mace with the other.

257.

A wooden book cover
Kangra Style,
early nineteenth century
$7\frac{7}{8} \times 12\frac{3}{8}$ inches

On the obverse, Sarasvatī, the Goddess of Learning, holds a lute and a book in the two upper hands. She is seated on a lotus placed on a striped carpet. On the reverse, the elephant-headed God Gaṇeśa sits on a throne and partakes of sweets offered to him on a tray. In a corner of the terrace is the mouse vehicle in a worshipful attitude.

258.

Guru Nānak's initiation
as a student
Pahāṛī Style,
early nineteenth century
$5\frac{3}{4} \times 5$ inches

The young Nānak stands facing the teacher, who is seated on a square stool, holding a wooden tablet in his hand. An ink pot and other writing materials lie at the side. In the foreground are several students at work and play. In the background is a hilly landscape, streaked with grass.

The painting preserves few characteristics of the Pahāṛī style, except in the treatment of mountains and trees, and may perhaps belong to a center in the Punjab plains.

259.

Entertainment during
the rainy season
Kangra Style,
mid-nineteenth century
$7\frac{3}{8} \times 9\frac{1}{4}$ inches

In a forest clearing has been set up a revolving wheel with chairs on which several ladies are amusing themselves. In a bower to the left are Kṛishṇa and Rādhā. The trees are loaded with flowering creepers and the clouded sky, streaked with lightning, is filled with flying cranes in geometric formation.

260.

Four illustrations to
an unidentified Ms.
Pahāṛī Style,
mid-nineteenth century
$8\frac{3}{4} \times 5\frac{1}{2}$ inches

(top left)
A lady bathes in a pool fed by a mountain stream. A couple standing in a palace observe her. A blazing sun rises in the sky.

(top right)
Lovers drinking. Dark clouds and

260

lightning in the sky. A row of rose flowers indicates the garden setting. Curious craggy, green mountains with flowers to the left.

(bottom left)

A couple, seated in a golden pavilion, are shown smoking a *hukkā*. Two ladies grill kababs in the foreground.

(bottom right)

The man, one arm around the shoulders of his lady, is plucking a pomegranate fruit. To the right is a decorative tree clasped by a vine yielding enormous bunches of grapes. In the foreground is a bitch suckling her young.

These small illustrations are done in a simple manner, but show a great deal of inventiveness in treating the elements of the landscape.

261.

Gulāb Singh (1820–1857)
Pahāṛī Style,
mid-nineteenth century
6 × 3¾ inches

The chief, wearing a red, embroidered coat, is seated on a chair with one hand resting on a sword. He is attended by a retainer waving a whisk.

The Sikhs, who succeeded in subduing the various hill chiefs, adopted the style of painting favored by the people whom they conquered.

Gulāb Singh, a Ḍogrā, served under Ranjīt Singh (1780–1839) and later became the ruler of Jammu.

262.

Rājā Dhiān Singh
Pahāṛī Style,
mid-nineteenth century
$9\frac{1}{8} \times 6\frac{1}{2}$ inches

The Rājā, on horseback, carries a hawk perched on his hand. He is attended by a parasol-bearer and a footman carrying a gun.

Dhiān Singh, the younger brother of Gulāb Singh (Cat. no. 261), rose to the highest rank and power under Ranjīt Singh, whose service he entered in 1822. He was assassinated in 1843.

263.

Folio from a Ms. of
the *Bhāgavata Daśamskandha*
by Kṛishṇadāsa
Kangra Style,
late nineteenth century
$3\frac{1}{4} \times 3\frac{1}{4}$ inches

The circular picture, placed in the center of the folio, shows the baby Kṛishṇa with his parents.

264–265.

Two folios from a series
illustrating the *Rāmāyaṇa*
Pahāṛī Style,
late nineteenth century
$8\frac{1}{4} \times 9\frac{1}{4}$ inches

(264.) Rāma, seated on a terrace, is shown playing *chaupaṛ* with Sītā who is getting ready to throw the dice. The hot greens and yellows, as well as other pigments, possess none of the mellowness of traditional colors and are examples of the aniline dyes that were being used by the traditional artists at this time.

(265.) Battle between Rāma and Rāvaṇa.

The adversaries are in combat; by virtue of a divine gift, Rāvaṇa grows back the limbs severed from his body.

266.

An embroidered *rumāl*
Chamba, nineteenth century
$28\frac{1}{2} \times 28\frac{1}{2}$ inches

In the central field is the *Rāsa* dance, the God Kṛishṇa alternating with a cowmaid, each of whom holds what looks like three tassels in a hand. Geese are shown along the inner edge of the beaded circle. The concentric margins are embroidered with floral arabesques.

267.

An embroidered *rumāl*
Chamba, early
nineteenth century
$22\frac{1}{2} \times 22\frac{3}{4}$ inches

Two rows, consisting of four panels each, are filled with motifs popular in Pahāṛī painting. These include Kṛishṇa coloring Rādhā's feet, women beneath trees, and other subjects. Floral arabesques fill the field and the margin.

South Indian Styles

Painting in South India has an extremely long tradition, but, aside from murals, most of the surviving examples are of fairly recent date. Images of divinities continue to be produced at the great temple cities, where they are purchased by pilgrims, usually for worship.

REFERENCE:
C. SIVARAMAMURTI, *South Indian Paintings* (New Delhi, 1968).

268.

Scenes from the *Rāmāyaṇa*
South India (probably Tanjore), eighteenth century
$6 \times 4\frac{5}{8}$ inches

The fragment formed part of a larger composition, the left half of which is missing. The space is divided into rectangular panels, each one of which is filled with a scene from the *Rāmāyaṇa*:

First register: Rāma in exile, attended by his allies.
Second register: Rāma receiving gifts; a chariot driving away.
Third register: Rāma with his allies before the walled city of Laṅkā.
Fourth register: Sītā undergoing the

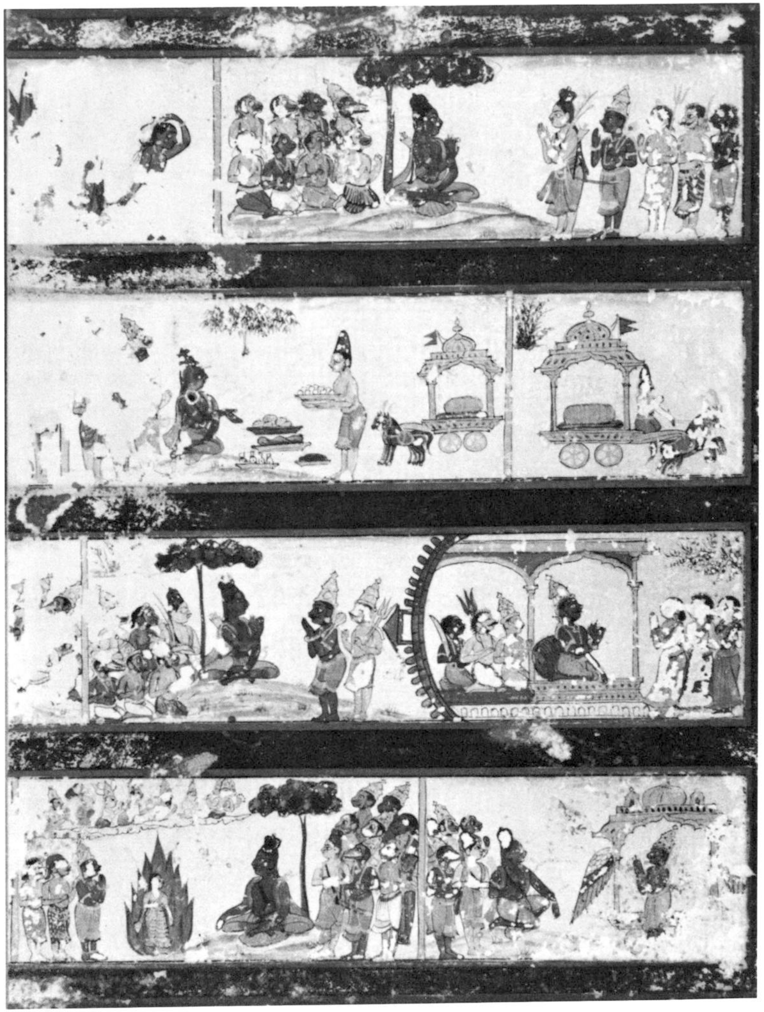

268

ordeal by fire; the arrival of the aerial chariot.

269.

The Goddess Sarasvatī
South India (Tanjore),
twentieth century
$13\frac{1}{2} \times 11\frac{1}{4}$ inches

The four-armed Goddess plays on the lute with two hands and holds a book and a string of beads in the others. She is seated on a throne backed by an enormous bolster and framed by a cusped arch.

Bits of colored glass and mirrors have been embedded into the lacquer in a technique which becomes very popular at this time.

270.

Shrines of Rāma and Vishṇu
South India,
late nineteenth century
$13\frac{1}{8} \times 17$ inches

In the temple to the left are images of Rāma accompanied by Sītā and the winged Garuḍa. In the temple to the right is Vishṇu lying on the serpent Śesha, and also an image of a standing Vishṇu flanked by his consorts and worshippers.

Bits of colored glass are embedded in the lacquered picture.

271.

Vishṇu and his incarnations
South India, twentieth century
$10\frac{1}{4} \times 8\frac{1}{4}$ inches

In the center, within an oval panel, is the cosmic form of the four-armed Vishṇu. Immediately above, in three medallions, is an image of Vishṇu flanked by Nārada and Tumburu, and immediately below is a seated Vishṇu with a *chaurī* bearer on either side. The other medallions contain the various incarnations. Beginning from the bottom left we have the Matsya (Fish), Kūrma (Turtle), Varāha (Boar), Nṛisiṁha (Man-Lion), and Vāmana (Dwarf) incarnations. From the top right we have Paraśurama, Balarāma, Rāma, Kṛishṇa, and the incarnation which is yet to come, Kalki.